THE SIRTFOOD DIET 2021

And

KETO DIET FOR WOMEN OVER 50

|2 BOOK IN 1|

The ultimate Guide for Reboot Your Metabolism Step-By-Step and Quickly Burn Fat.

Get Healthy Again, Balance your Hormones and Find your Best Shape with the Comprehensive Ketogenic Guide and sirftood diet.

| May 2021 Edition|

Table Of Contents

THE

SIRTFOOD

DIET 2021

The Essential Sirtfood Diet That Shocked the Celebrity's World. The Revolutionary Plan to Activate Your Skinny Gene to Lose Weight, Stay Lean & Feel Fit. Includes 28 Days Meal Plan.

| May 2021 Edition|

Legal & Disclaimer

Introduction to the Sirtfood Diet

Sirtfoods are a recently discovered group of nutrient rich foods which seem to be able to 'activate' the body's skinny genes (also known as sirtuins), in much the same way as fasting diets do, with the same range of benefits, but without the common downsides of fasting diets, such as hunger, irritability and muscle loss.

By eating a diet rich in Sirtfoods, it is claimed that participants will lose weight, gain muscle, look and feel better and maybe even live a longer and more healthy life. The Sirtfood Diet was created by nutritionists Aiden Goggins and Glen Matten. They were so interested by the potential of Sirtfoods, they created a diet based around maximising Sirtfood intake and mild calorie restriction. They then tested this diet on participants from an exclusive London gym and were amazed by their findings. Gym members lost an average of 7lbs in the first 7 days, despite not increasing their levels of exercise. Not only did the participants lose a substantial amount of weight, but they also gained muscle (usually the opposite happens when dieting) and reported significant improvements in overall health and well-being. What sounds like a snack lifted straight from a sci-fi movie, a 'sirtfood' is actually a food high in sirtuin activators, says nutritionist Rob Hobson. Sirtuins are a type of protein which protect the cells in our bodies from dying or becoming inflamed through illness, though research has also shown they can help regulate your metabolism, increase muscle and burn fat, hence the new 'wonderfood' tag. Sirtfoods are mostly plant-based and high in antioxidants that help trick your body into burning fat at a higher rate. It's called Sirt because it includes eating foods that are high in sirtuin activators, defined as seven proteins found in the body that regulate metabolism, inflammation, and the longevity of cells.

The basic and essential principles you need to know About Weight and Fat Loss

These days almost everyone is concerned with losing weight or more importantly losing fat. I am asked more questions about this topic than all others and it is an obvious source of confusion for many people. The problem is there are many different opinions about the best

way to lose fat and most have at least some truth to them.

One popular strategy suggests concentrating on the percentage of calories from fat that you burn during the exercise. This leads to recommendations for exercising at a particular intensity/heart rate, which is often called the fat burning zone. This sounds like a good way to figure out how to exercise for maximal fat burning, but when you exercise to burn the highest percentage of fat, you end up burning fewer total calories, because the exercise intensity is too low.

Another common strategy is to focus on the total number of calories burned during your workout instead of the actual fat calories. This is recommended because unless you burn more calories throughout the day than you consume, you will never lose fat, regardless of the percentage of calories you burn while exercising. This is true, but just looking at the number or type of calories burned while exercising never gives you the full story.

There are however other important factors that are often overlooked when determining how to exercise for optimal fat loss. First, some types of exercise, such as resistance training, may not burn a lot of calories during the actual workout, but your body will keep burning calories at a higher rate for many hours after you stop exercising. This increased calorie burning effect will vary depending on the duration, intensity, and type of exercise.

As a result, it becomes very difficult to accurately determine how many calories are really burned due to your workout.

Fortunately, knowing how many calories or how much fat you burn while exercising is not as important as you might think. The real issue is how your workout affects your metabolism. Increasing your metabolism is by far the most beneficial thing you can do to improve long-term fat loss. Your metabolism is responsible for burning many more calories than exercise and if your main goal is fat loss, you should focus on increasing your metabolism as much as possible.

Increasing the body's metabolism is a complicated issue that is affected by genetics, exercise, nutrition, and a number of other lifestyle factors. Since this article is about exercise and this issue is too large to be properly addressed in this article, I will concentrate on a basic strategy to help improve your metabolism.

This strategy essentially has 2 main goals, preventing muscle loss and challenging your body. Muscle has a significant influence on your metabolic rate and every pound of muscle burns about 30 calories per day. If you stop doing exercises that stress your muscles, you will start losing muscle and your metabolism will slow down. Moderate to high intensity resistance training (weights, bodyweight exercises, etc.) is an ideal choice for this type of workout.

As a general rule, you should perform exercises that are difficult enough that you are unable to perform 15 reps; 6 to 12 reps per exercise is a good range. This may be more intense than your usual workout, but if you only have enough time for a short workout, it will be enough intensity to retain your current level of muscle. Also, since your exercise time will be short and the number of total sets will be low, you shouldn't have to worry about gaining muscle or bulking up. Bodybuilders have large muscles mainly because they perform an excessive number of sets, sometimes 20-30 per muscle group, not because they lift heavier weights.

The overall workout only needs to be 15-30 minutes long and you have some options as to how to design the workout. You can do 1 set of many different exercises, multiple sets of a few exercises or anything in between. With the increased intensity of the exercises, you probably won't want to exercise much longer anyway.

A higher percentage of leg exercises (squats, lunges, etc.) than usual is also suggested. This is because your largest muscles are in your legs and exercises that stress large muscles create a greater overall demand on the body and produce better metabolic improvements. Try for 35 - 40 % leg exercises if your workout is 30 minutes and around 50% if the workout is closer to 15 minutes. This approach will also maximize the number of calories burned during the workout and result in more calories being burned throughout the day.

If you would rather perform endurance activities (running, biking, etc.), you can apply the same principles of increasing the intensity to make the exercise more demanding. Perhaps the best method is to replace a constant intensity aerobic workout with a shorter interval training workout. This involves alternating between your normal pace and much more challenging pace. For example if you are a runner, you could alternate between running for 1 minute at your regular speed and sprinting for 30 seconds.

Regardless of which approach you take, you should feel about as fatigued at the end of your short workout as you do after a regular length workout. However, if you are not accustomed to more intense training, it is important to start out slowly and let your body adapt to the training. It is very important not to overdo it or push yourself too hard. You want to feel fatigued, but not run down or excessively sore. Also, even though the workout is short, you still need to warm up before the workout and stretch/cool down after you finish.

Keep in mind this strategy does not represent a complete well-rounded fitness program and is not intended to replace your existing program. It is especially useful during times when you may have a limited amount of time to exercise, such as while traveling and it is also beneficial for adding variety to your program. I chose this approach so people with different workout routines and overall goals could apply the strategy to their individual situations.

Look at your existing program and determine how to apply this information to benefit your most. In addition, be sure to remember that nutrition and lifestyle factors (sleep, stress, etc.) are always important too. You can have the best exercise program in the world and if you have bad nutrition and lifestyle habits you will still have a hard time losing fat

Before getting into any diet or workout program, you have to first understand how your bodily process works. The body has the ability to perform its daily function with a calorie maintenance level. The appropriate amount of calories enables you to walk around and maintain the inner bodily functions. Calories are the body's source of power. Without the proper quantity of calories, you'll feel sick.

The calories we need are from our drinking and eating habits. Weight does not go up or decrease when we eat the same number of calories fit for our daily requirements. Demonstrating this explanation: if your maintenance amount is 3000 calories and you eat an equal amount a day, you will not increase your weight. Weight increases when we consume more than our calorie maintenance level. The opposite, which is weight loss, occurs when we use up the daily maintenance level. We can also reduce calories by eating fewer from our everyday maintenance level. Hence, an individual with a 3000 calorie maintenance quantity should eat 2500 calories to reduce weight.

At this moment, you'd want to understand your calorie maintenance level. Your maintenance level is computed by using the Basal Metabolic Rate (BMR) of the Harris-Benedict Equation. The body's BMR is the quantity of calories you need to eat to maintain executing your daily responsibilities. How much activity you perform is considered when computing the calories you have to burn per day. You can look for everyday calorie maintenance level calculators online to understand what your body needs.

Now that you have comprehended the principle behind weight reduction, it's time to know the fundamental ways to lose weight. These 3 essential ways are all you require. The first is to work out. Exercise allows you to burn more calories. If you commit to your daily calories maintenance level, you'll end up losing that same amount. Thus, no weight change happens. But if you'd want to reduce weight, you'll have to engage in exercise that loses a greater amount from your calories maintenance level. With the past example, you will have to reduce additional 500 calories for weight loss.

Aside from exercise, you will also have to eat lesser of your daily maintenance amount. Those with a 3000 maintenance amount will have to sacrifice 500 calories and just eat 2500. A caloric deficit occurs as you give your body a lesser amount of the calories it needs for maintenance. Engaging in more of caloric shortages will give the body consistent weight loss.

The safest and most recommended method of weight loss requires both diet and exercise. Eating less calories and burning more calories gives the body a stability of what's gained and lost from your activities. It's been confirmed consistently that a healthy diet and workouts will give you quicker and long lasting weight loss results. Employing both methods are also the proper means and doesn't get in the way of your daily responsibilities.

Before you get into a workout routine or diet, you first must analyze your body's maintenance level. The analysis will be your form's adjustment into a better routine. Begin by eating your calorie maintenance level regularly for each day. Sustain such caloric consumption for 2 to three weeks. It doesn't have to be the same quantity of calories, as long as it is|comes very close. To ensure you're eating the appropriate quantity, weigh yourself once a week (before eating and on an empty stomach) in the day's beginning.

If you had a weight consistent for the two to 3 weeks, then you were able to eat the calories needed of your maintenance level. In order for you to reduce more weight, you must eat 500 less of your daily maintenance level per day. If your maintenance level is 2500, you will have to start consuming only 2000 calories a day.

Those who were unable to keep up their calorie maintenance level can still start a healthy weight reduction program. All you have to do is consume 500 less of your maintenance level and redo the body adjustment with the smaller calories quantity. If you were successful in eating the lessened maintenance level, then you must begom consuming minus 500 again of the initial amount.

It is important for one to ensure you do not lose the weight too fast. Reducing weight at a dangerous rate will compromise your well being. If you catch yourself losing three or more pounds each week regularly for some weeks in a row, then you'll have to make certain adjustments. The adjustment involves including 250 to 300 calories to your daily consumption. After which, you have to start watching your weight with the new quantity. Remember, you shouldn't just eat a smaller amount. You need to exercise to reduce enough calories for healthy weight reduction.

The prescribed weight reduction speed is around one to 2 pounds per week. Remember, reducing weight very quickly won't benefit your body. You have to maintain a loss speed that will continue to keep you fit. Your health is much more important than looking good. Our physique cannot catch up with very quick weight loss. In fact, it will simply change to stay alive if you quicken the procedure. Instead, body fat will be kept so it can catch up. Hence, you must only stick to shedding one to 2 pounds a week. If you're capable of doing so for one year, you'll eventually lose fifty to 100 pounds!

As we have already covered the calculations, it's time to get to the specifics. What type of meals should you be consuming? What must you avoid at all costs?

Let us start with the positive side. There's many delicious food out there that still allows you sustain and lose weight. Do not fall for fad diets that pretend low carbs or no fats will offer you the best outcome. These diets are only out to get profit from your desperation. A healthy physique requires all foods. You just have to balance them accordingly. The best experts to talk about meal choices with are physicians and nutritionists. They're give value for your money and are only looking out for your health.

A decent diet will entail the proper quantity of fats, carbohydrates, and proteins. An average healthy adult requires 30 % of their calorie intake to be from fat. So, if you consume 2000 calories daily, 400 to 600 calories will be from fat. Since 9 calories is found in 1 gram of fat, you'll have to consume 44 to 66 grams each day for the average person.

The best sources of fat are nuts, seeds, olive and canola oil, avocados, fish, fish oil, and flax seed oil formulas. Weight reducers should note that fat really does not make you "fat" if it comes from the healthy foods. Fat will not get in the way of your weight loss. It'll only contribute to your health and enhance your endurance. As long as you get your fat from the mentioned sources, you will not have to worry.

Another infamous food types for fad dieters is carbohydrates. It's advised that 50 % of your calorie intake are eaten from carbs. The conversion you have to recall: one gram of carbohydrates is four calories. Hence, someone who consumes 2000 calories per day will have to eat a thousand from carbohydrates. Thus, you have to consume 250 grams from carbohydrates a day. The healthies sources of carbs are fruits, sweet potatoes, beans, vegetables, oatmeal, and brown rice. In other words, eat complex carbohydrates and not the simple carbs. Simple carbohydrates are from sugary food like white rice, white bread, soda, and other highly processed foods.

As for protein, the recommended minimum daily amount is 0.8 grams for every kg of your body weight. To compute for this, divide your weight by 2.2 then multiply by 0.8.

Since such is merely the minimum, people who participate in workouts should consume more than the computed amount. You can eat a bit more to assure your safety. The best choices of protein are turkey, chicken, fish, lean meats, eggs/egg whites, nuts, and beans.

Let us proceed to the meals you have to avoid. Most of these foods are obviously very bad for your well being. The basics to not eat are soft drinks, fast food, candy, cookies, crackers, cakes, pastries, and chips. Aside from these, don't eat food with Trans and saturated fat. Stay away from meals that have increased sodium and sugar levels. These meals||foods are usually where you get your extra calories. Aside from the added pounds, you will push yourself towards an unhealthy lifestyle.

Now that we have discussed the diet, it's time to discuss exercise. Working out is the best way for you to burn calories. Besides weight loss, it will also enhance||improve] your power, flexibility, and endurance. For the long run, it will also help you in preventing heart diseases and bone deteriorations.

There are 2 kinds of exercise for you to engage in: aerobic and anaerobic. Aerobic exercise is more renowned as the cardiovascular workouts. Cardio workouts enhance your cardiovascular endurance, done at a lasting pace in minimal to average forces. Cardio activities are walking, skating, jogging, swimming, biking, and elliptical machine activities. The most prescribed cardiology exercise is one that you enjoy and are eager to participate in habitually. Those who enjoy walking should do a daily walk. Bikers can continue with their pastime while swimming is perfect for water lovers. In terms of their time, the recommended schedule is thirty minutes. Those who can stillcarry on above it can still prolong. However, the thirty minutes is recommended for the average person. Do the cardio workout for about three to six days per week.

Anaerobic exercise puts focus on your muscle and stamina. These are typically weight training, calisthenics (like pushups), and using resistance machines. Anaerobic workouts burn you a notable quantity of calories. Although it is not as many as cardio workouts, they will enhance your stamina for the cardioexercises. It will also contribute very positive looks on your body. The increase of muscle will make you appear more toned and sexy. The advise speed of anaerobic exercises is between two to 4 times a week.

There are also some diet legends everyone must disregard. The first is the misconception consuming fat and carbohydrates makes you fat. Didn't we just state that fat and carbs are important to a person's health? You need these food types for your calories maintenance level. The next are those silly and useless one- meal diets. Just eating a small celery or cabbage soup will just kill you. Just eating one tiny food will not burn your fat. Your body will simply respond to the lack of food and sustain your current fat.

Another myth is that spot reduction workouts allow you to lose all your fats. Focusing on a single area is not the answer. This is because workouts focus on your muscles. If the muscles are sealed by fat, they will continue to be hidden. You'll have to reduce that fat for your muscles to show.

The most obvious fallacies are those products sold in infomercials. People do not lose their fat by relying on one sole product. Same goes with those ab machines. Such machines are only another instance of spot reduction. Any other fast or easy means to weight reduction is just out to get your money. You have to accept that weight loss entails perseverance and a large amount of your time.

If you want to invest cash for your weight loss, you should avail of a gym membership. Gyms have machines for both aerobic and anaerobic exercises. It is also a helpful motivator. You would not want to spend your money and not use that membership. You are also motivated by the individuals with you. Other means that will help you in weight reduction: digital food scale, treadmill, bike, elliptical machine, weights, tape measure, and a body weight scale.

In terms of your diet, you need to eat smaller foods more habitually. It is not recommended to eat one to three big meals a day. Instead, break it down into five to six small meals. Consume the meals every 2 to 3 hours. Another method to enhance your diet is to arrange your meals. Plan it on the beginning of the week and cook them early. This way, you are not bpunded by the fatty meals sold in restaurants or fast food places. You should also take your food with water. Drink it as you consume the meal. The water will make you full faster and stop you from consuming additional calories. Don't eat very fast. Your body will take some time to absorb that it is becoming full. Grind the food gradually and don't eat in a rush. If you eat too quickly, you'll consume more than your body actually requires.

Everybody wants to lose pounds. This is one fact that is manifestly supported by the countless weight loss programs in the market, together with the countless weight loss products, ranging from snack bars, powdered juices, shakes and even to slimming soaps and lotions! It can really be confusing making an attempt to understand which ones are for real and which of them are junk, especially when presented with all these information.

You Don't have To Practice Everything

It's not particularly necessary that you know wholeheartedly all the available diets out in the market. In fact, most of them can have conflicting principles. For instance, one would say that you need to eat a lot of little meals throughout the day, while another would say that you should only eat one large meal for the day and starve yourself till you start another day. Confusing isn't it? You need to research to find out which information is the real thing and which of them are not.

So, here are the necessary things you need to know about weight loss before you decide to endure any sort of diet program.

Losing Weight Is Not Instant

Although it might truly be glorious if you might shed weight straight away shortly after away shortly after employing a product, sadly you'd have to face the reality that losing weight is not an instant process. Don't be fooled with the countless diet programs and products that make 5-minute guarantees. Losing weight is rarely instant, unless you're undergoing liposuction surgery.

You should understand that it is a process that takes quite a long amount of time for it to be effective. There are really no shortcuts here. Unless you impose real discipline to yourself, in regard to eating healthy and living a healthy lifestyle, you would not lose weight on an everlasting basis.

Weight Loss Involves Activity

There are so many diet programs and each of them varies with their underlying beliefs. Watching what you eat is good. There is nothing wrong with that. However, you should keep in mind that food isn't the only factor that you should consider when trying to lose weight. Another crucial factor would be your body's activity.

If you need to shed some fat and make your diet effective, you should couple your food monitoring with the right exercise. Dieting want really work when you're living the life of a couch potato or you're simply in bed for the entire work when you are Living a couch potato or lifestyle will do you no good.

Starvation Is Not The Answer

Going on a hunger strike will not answer your fat issues. Believing in the popular belief that starving your body will make you shed pounds is a common mistake by many people. At first, this principle may make sense, it doesn't really work that simple.

If the body senses starvation, it automatically many folks. Initially, this as a signal for stress. When under stress, the body does automatic actions, such as production of hormones to negate this stress. In this situation, it produces more of cortisol, which is a vital hormone that excites fat production. Additionally, your body will keep more water. When it starts water retention, this will definitely add to your body weight, since the body is especially composed from water.

Metabolism Varies

Metabolism is how fast or slow your body gets use from the food you eat and turn them into energy. You should understand that people do not have the body is especially consisting of metabolism. People have varied rates, and this may really affect how prone an individual is for gaining weight. Generally, people with slow metabolism are prone to gain weight simply. Those with folk don't have the ones that may eat a lot yet still don't get fat. This is a good reason why eating what your chum eats within the day wouldn't necessarily lead you to ones that slim body that she has. You may have different metabolic rates, which makes it okay for her to eat one entire box of pizza inside in the day without troubling of getting fat, while you get to eat all greens, that she has.

What you need to know about weight loss

In today's society, weight loss is becoming a more popular fad by the day. It has become the focus point of many conversations, the infamous New Year's resolution and the first worry before swimsuit season. However, most are shocked to realize that shedding those extra pounds are not as easy as first imagined. Many face problems because they are not educated about weight loss. In order to succeed, one must understand the concept behind achieving a healthier lifestyle.

What is Healthy Weight?

The most important goal should be to reach a healthy weight. Healthy weight is the weight ones body becomes when he/she eats a nutritious diet consistently, are physically active and balance the calorie intake with his/her physical activity. Being at this healthy weight can reduce of type two diabetes, high blood pressure, stroke, heart disease and certain types of cancer. To achieve a healthy weight, a physician should be consulted to create a weight loss program that is suited for the individual.

Difficulty with Losing Weight

If there are so many programs and techniques available, then why is losing weight so hard? Most weight loss is difficult because there are so many factors involved. Weight is influenced by genetics, metabolism, personal behavior, environment and culture. When considering all of these factors, it becomes a challenge to obtain the correct balance for weight loss. Most have better results when they shift to a healthier lifestyle than targeting weight loss alone. The main goal here is to develop healthier eating habits and combining them with regular physical activity. Creating healthy habits produces better long-term results than bouncing around from one diet to another.

Getting Started

Once the decision has been made to lose weight, it is important to maintain certain ideas throughout the process. The goal should be to achieve better health, not to lose so many pounds by the end of the week. Also remember that the change does not have to be made all at once. Making small changes to one's daily routine can make significant improvements in his/her health. To be successful in making lifestyle changes, remember key points: don't diet, think about the relationship with food, slowly change eating habits, establish realistic goals and make physical a part of daily routine.

Losing weight is not only about appearance. It is about trying to create a healthier way of living. Weight control is a life-long effort and must be taken seriously. By implementing healthy changes and a positive attitude, one can be on the way to a successful weight loss.

How to Use Sirtfoods to Burn fat

One major reason the sirtfood diet has exploded in popularity is due to its allowance of dark chocolate and red wine, as both items are considered sirtfoods. The claim is that by focusing on these foods, rapid weight loss will follow without decreases in muscle mass. A sirtfood dieter will begin their first week drinking green juice made of matcha green tea, lemon juice, parsley, celery, a green apple and arugula three times per week. After the first week, sirtfood dieters return to eating three meals per day made only with sirtfoods and will continue to incorporate these foods throughout the remainder of the diet.

The latest diet cleanse which has got the world raving about it follows a scientific approach to battle weight gain.

The diet popularises on the use of 'sirtfoods', which are some special foods which work by activating certain protein chains in the body, known as sirtuins. According to science, these antioxidant agents act as protectants that help slow down aging, boost metabolism and regulate the body's inflammation, hereby helping in fat loss.

Studies have also found that the sirtfood diet can help people lose up to seven pounds (3 kilos) in under a week's time.

As complex and scientific as this diet plan sounds, the diet encourages you to include some of the most commonly found kitchen ingredients as well as some indulgent foods. Some common foods allowed in this plan include foods like oranges, dark chocolates, parsley, turmeric, kale, and even red wine.

The diet, though considered to be a fad, focusses on maintaining a restrictive weight loss strategy one week. While the first three days makes you limit your calorie intake to 1000kcal (consuming three sirt food green juices and having a meal). The remaining days, you are allowed to increase your calorie intake to 1500kcal and have two meals a day (along with two sirtfood juices). Post this, the maintenance phase recommends you to eat up to three balanced foods rich in sirtuin, coupled with an effective workout strategy to lose weight, making it all the more sustainable.

Since it is rather restrictive in nature, many stay wary of the diet plan working in the long run. The diet restricts your calorie intake and can devoid you of other needed nutrients, so, it is not a long term, sustainable diet plan for weight loss.

There seems to be a growing number of celebrities and notable figures who've touted the sirtfood diet for their recent weight loss success. However, consumers must keep in mind that celebrities often have access to professional support when it comes to what they consume and any additional exercise regimens. Additionally, studies on the efficacy of this diet are slim. Granted, most foods listed are healthy whole food options and calorie restrictions which are automatically connected to some weight loss. The majority of foods listed have anti-inflammatory properties, high amounts of antioxidants and nutrients which are of course, beneficial. Medical experts warn though, that while quick weight loss is possible on such a diet, a majority of that initial loss will be water weight. It may also be risky for those who engage in moderate to high physical activity.

So how does the sirtfood diet works

The diet is split into 2 phases. Phase 1: the 7 day 'hypersuccess phase', which combines a Sirtfood-rich diet with moderate calorie restriction, and Phase 2: the 14 day 'maintenance phase', where you consolidate your weight loss without restricting calories.

PHASE 1 OF THE SIRTFOOD DIET

During the first 3 days, calorie intake is restricted to 1,000 calories (so, still more than on a 5:2 fasting day). The diet consists of 3 Sirtfood-rich green juices and 1 Sirtfood-rich meal and 2 squares of dark chocolate.

During the remaining 4 days, calorie intake is increased to 1, 500 calories and each day the diet comprises 2 Sirtfood-rich green juices and 2 Sirtfood-rich meals.

During phase 1 you are not allowed to drink any alcohol, but you can drink water, tea, coffee and green tea freely.

PHASE 2 OF THE SIRTFOOD DIET

Phase 2 does not focus on calorie restriction. Each day involves 3 Sirtfood-rich meals and 1 green juice, plus the option of 1 or 2 Sirtfood bite snacks, if required.

In phase 2 you are allowed to drink red wine, but in moderation (the recommendation is 2-3 glasses of red wine per week), as well as water, tea, coffee and green tea.

Phase two lasts for two weeks. During this "maintenance" phase, you should continue to steadily lose weight.

There is no specific calorie limit for this phase. Instead, you eat three meals full of sirtfoods and one green juice per day.

After the Diet

You may repeat these two phases as often as desired for further weight loss. However, you are encouraged to continue "sirtifying" your diet after completing these phases by incorporating sirtfoods regularly into your meals.

There are a variety of Sirtfood Diet books that are full of recipes rich in sirtfoods. You can also include sirtfoods in your diet as a snack or in recipes you already use. Additionally, you are encouraged to continue drinking the green juice every day. In this way, the Sirtfood Diet becomes more of a lifestyle change than a one-time diet.

How to do the sirtfood diet

Though the diet is often hailed as easy to follow thanks to the fact it includes red wine and dark chocolate, it's fairly strict in its guidelines.

The sirtfood plan relies on dieters restricting their calorie intake as well as eating a specific list of foods that are said to boost the metabolism.

The three-week plan involves an initial seven-day phase, followed by two weeks on phase two, AKA the "maintenance" phase.

One of the key components is a green juice which the founders call "rocket fuel", which followers of the diet have to make up to three times a day.

Sirtfood green juice recipe

- 75 grams (2.5 oz) kale
- 30 grams (1 oz) arugula (rocket)
- 5 grams parsley
- 2 celery sticks
- 1 cm (0.5 in) ginger
- half a green apple
- half a lemon
- half a teaspoon matcha green tea

Using a blender, juice all of the ingredients except for the green tea powder and lemon together, and pour them into a glass. Juice the lemon by hand, then stir both the lemon juice and green tea powder in.

This juice is important for phase one, which is designed to jump-start the weight loss. It involves restricting calories to just 1,000 a day (which is below the recommended daily intake).

Anyone following the plan would have three green juices per day plus one meal.

In the last three days of that initial week, the calorie intake increases to 1,500 a day, so you can add two more meals and have just two juices.

The recipes are all laid out in the official book, and include meals such as omelettes, salads and stir fries.

In phase two, dieters can then enjoy three sirtfood-rich meals and one sirtfood green juice a day, rather than watching the calorie count.

According to the founders, you should lose weight steadily throughout the plan.

A complete List of Healthy and Delicious Foods You can use every day

Losing weight can be challenging and there are so many choices, it's hard to sometimes decide what is healthy and what isn't. If you are looking for a sample of a food menu and need to know which foods are the best, then read on. Here you will learn about 10 foods which can be a dieter's best friend.

Low-Fat Cottage Cheese

Low-fat cottage cheese can make a huge difference to anyone looking to shed a few pounds. It's low in fat, carbs and calories, while remaining high in protein. One-half cup of cottage cheese contains 15 grams of protein, nearly the same as 2 ounces of poultry, fish or cooked lean meat.

Cottage cheese is also very versatile, so if you don't care for the taste by itself, you can add in fresh fruit to sweeten it up a bit.

There are very few foods which are as healthy as cottage cheese. In addition to the aforementioned benefits, low-fat cottage cheese is also loaded up with Vitamin D and calcium, both which contribute to a healthy lifestyle.

Eggs

Eggs, like low-fat cottage cheese, are low in fat but high in protein. The fat that eggs do have is the right kind of fat. From the 5 grams of fat per egg, only 1.5 grams is saturated fat. If you're worried about cholesterol, don't be quick to dismiss eggs. The American Heart Association acknowledges that an egg a day is acceptable as long as you limit dietary cholesterol from other sources.

Many experts believe that saturated fats and trans fats have a bigger impact that dietary cholesterol in raising blood cholesterol. Eating an egg will make you feel fuller and curb your cravings for unhealthy snacks. Next time, why not reach for an egg instead of the chips.

Blueberries

By now, most people have heard about the many benefits of eating blueberries. Luckily, they are readily available and great for a mid-morning or a mid-afternoon snack when you need an energy boost. Blueberries contain load of antioxidants, which are thought to be important in reducing free radicals that can cause cancer and speed up the aging process.

According to researchers from the USDA Human Nutrition Center, blueberries are ranked number 1 in antioxidant activity when compared with 40 other fresh fruits and vegetables. Blueberries are perfect for the dieter because they are tasty, low in calories and high in nutrition.

Walnuts

These are among the healthiest foods you can eat. Rich in fiber, magnesium, B vitamins and antioxidants like Vitamin E, they are also one of these best plant sources of protein. Walnuts have also been shown to lower LDL cholesterol (the bad kind).

Since nuts in general are high in fat, eating in moderation is the key. About 20 walnut halves (equivalent to 1.5 oz per day) is about the recommended serving of these tasty treats. Walnuts can be eaten alone as a snack or as toppers for salads, pasta, oatmeal and an almost infinite variety of dishes.

Spinach

Rich in vitamin C, fiber, carotenoids and iron, spinach is a nutritional powerhouse. Known to protect against cancer and heart disease, it's hard to beat this food. Spinach is tasty as a side dish (sautéed in a bit of olive oil and garlic) or as a foundation for a great salad. It's naturally low in calories and is high in flavor as well as nutritious.

Sweet Potatoes

These naturally sweet vegetables are tasty and available almost year-round. Sweet potatoes have significant antioxidant qualities, in addition to being excellent sources of Vitamin A and Vitamin C. They also help fight inflammation and can help with diseases such as asthma and rheumatoid arthritis.

Sweet potatoes keep you feeling full for hours, which make the calories worthwhile. Sweet potatoes also have a low glycemic index, which means it breaks down slowly during digestion. It has been shown that lowering the glycemic load of the diet appears to be an effective method of promoting weight loss.

If you have a sugar craving, consider having a warm, baked sweet potato to curb your sweet tooth.

Watermelon

This tasty summer fruit is rich in potassium and Vitamin C. Watermelon is also a very good source of lycopene, which is preventative for a variety of cancers.

Watermelon is naturally low in calories, so it's the perfect no-guilt treat. If you're hungry for something fresh, juicy and sweet, watermelon is a great choice.

Salmon

Loaded with omega 3 fatty acids, this delicious pink fish can be served in a multitude of ways. Salmon contains a significant amount of the important omega 3 essential fatty acids, which are important in reducing unwanted inflammation and keeping our immune and circulatory systems healthy.

Salmon has plenty of protein, so it's filling and healthy to boot. Definitely a winning food!

Goji Berries

Although you might not be familiar with this tasty berry, it's so packed with vitamins, nutrients and protein, it is definitely a winning food.

These berries, also known as wolfberries, contain 18 kinds of amino acids, have more Vitamin C than oranges, more beta carotene than carrots and more iron than steak. Along with the ability to protect skin from sun damage they also help fight heart disease.

Goji berries can help in weight loss because they are high in fiber and also have a low glycemic index. They can be enjoyed as a snack by themselves, or in tea, juice, bars of cereal.

These berries are jam-packed with health benefits and are certainly worth a try.

Oatmeal

A large number of studies have shown that eating oatmeal can lower your cholesterol and help reduce your chance of heart disease. In addition, recent studies are showing that oatmeal may also help reduce the risk of type 2 diabetes. For those reasons, oatmeal should be a regular part of a healthy diet.

For a dieter, oatmeal can also help you lose weight. The soluble fiber in oatmeal absorbs a large amount of water which slows down the digestive process, making you feel full longer.

Top sirtfoods: 20 foods that activate weight loss.

Sirt foods help signal the body that it should rev up your metabolism and increase muscle mass while you burn fat. Also known as superfoods, the top 20 sirtfoods include the list below. Note that everyone gets excited about the wine and chocolate but your body is actually consistently eating more fiber, more antioxidants, and nutrient-dense foods.

- Kale
- Red wine
- Strawberries
- Onions
- Garlic
- Soy
- Parsley
- Extra virgin olive oil
- Dark chocolate (85% cocoa)
- Matcha green tea
- Buckwheat
- Turmeric
- Walnuts
- Arugula (rocket)
- Bird's eye chili (peppers)
- Lovage (herb)
- Medjool dates
- Red chicory
- Blueberries
- Capers
- Coffee

How to Start:

Week 1 - On the Sirtfood diet means you limit your calorie intake to 1,000 calories a day and drink three Sirtfood green juices throughout the day. The ingredients of a Sirtfood green juice are: Kale, arugula, parsley, celery, including the leaves, half a green apple, the juice of half of a lemon, and matcha green tea (we like. You can have it over ice or add water but don't add plant-based milk or other ingredients not on the list above.

Week 2 - You should increase calories to 1,500 a day and only drink two of the Sirtfood Juices a day, plus have two sirtfood meals each day. Continue on this pattern until you have lost the healthy amount of weight that your body needs to feel your best.

The healthy slow and steady weight loss will add up. If you lose 2 to 3 pounds a week that means you'll have lost 15 pounds in five weeks. Keep in mind that losing weight isn't a fast process and it wouldn't happen overnight, so if you have more than a small amount to lose, just tell yourself that consistency is the key, in order to sustain it over time.

Are Sirtfoods the New Superfoods?

There's no denying that sirtfoods are good for you. They are often high in nutrients and full of healthy plant compounds.

Moreover, studies have associated many of the foods recommended on the Sirtfood Diet with health benefits. For example, eating moderate amounts of dark chocolate with a high cocoa content may lower the risk of heart disease and help fight inflammation. Drinking green tea may reduce the risk of stroke and diabetes and help lower blood pressure.

And turmeric has anti-inflammatory properties that have beneficial effects on the body in general and may even protect against chronic, inflammation-related diseases. In fact, the majority of sirtfoods have demonstrated health benefits in humans. However, evidence on the health benefits of increasing sirtuin protein levels is preliminary. Yet, research in animals and cell lines have shown exciting results.

For example, researchers have found that increased levels of certain sirtuin proteins lead to longer lifespan in yeast, worms and mice. And during fasting or calorie restriction, sirtuin proteins tell the body to burn more fat for energy and improve insulin sensitivity. One study in mice found that increased sirtuin levels led to fat loss. Some evidence suggests that sirtuins may also play a role in reducing inflammation, inhibiting the development of tumors and slowing the development of heart disease and Alzheimer's.

While studies in mice and human cell lines have shown positive results, there have been no human studies examining the effects of increasing sirtuin levels. Therefore, whether increasing sirtuin protein levels in the body will lead to longer lifespan or a lower risk of cancer in humans is unknown. Research is currently underway to develop compounds effective at increasing sirtuin levels in the body. This way, human studies can begin to examine the effects of sirtuins on human health.

Until then, it's not possible to determine the effects of increased sirtuin levels.

Is It Healthy and Sustainable?

Sirtfoods are almost all healthy choices and may even result in some health benefits due to their antioxidant or anti-inflammatory properties. Yet eating just a handful of particularly healthy foods cannot meet all of your body's nutritional needs. The Sirtfood Diet is unnecessarily restrictive and offers no clear, unique health benefits over any other type of diet.

Furthermore, eating only 1,000 calories is typically not recommended without the supervision of a physician. Even eating 1,500 calories per day is excessively restrictive for many people. The diet also requires drinking up to three green juices per day. Although juices can be a good source of vitamins and minerals, they are also a source of sugar and contain almost none of the healthy fiber that whole fruits and vegetables do.

What's more, sipping on juice throughout the whole day is a bad idea for both your blood sugar and your teeth.

Not to mention, because the diet is so limited in calories and food choice, it is more than likely deficient in protein, vitamins and minerals, especially during the first phase. Due to the low calorie levels and restrictive food choices, this diet may be difficult to stick to for the entire three weeks. Add that to the high initial costs of having to purchase a juicer, the book and certain rare and expensive ingredients, as well as the time costs of preparing specific meals and juices, and this diet becomes unfeasible and unsustainable for many people.

Safety and Side Effects

Although the first phase of the Sirtfood Diet is very low in calories and nutritionally incomplete, there are no real safety concerns for the average, healthy adult considering the diet's short duration.

Yet for someone with diabetes, calorie restriction and drinking mostly juice for the first few days of the diet may cause dangerous changes in blood sugar levels.

Nevertheless, even a healthy person may experience some side effects, mainly hunger. Eating only 1,000–1,500 calories per day will leave just about anyone feeling hungry, especially if much of what you're consuming is juice, which is low in fiber, a nutrient that helps keep you feeling full. During phase one, you might experience other side effects such as fatigue, lightheadedness and irritability due to the calorie restriction. For the otherwise healthy adult, serious health consequences are unlikely if the diet is followed for only three week

The Bottom Line

The Sirtfood Diet is full of healthy foods, but not healthy eating patterns.

Not to mention, its theory and health claims are based on grand extrapolations from preliminary scientific evidence.

While adding some sirtfoods to your diet is not a bad idea and may even offer some health benefits, the diet itself looks like just another fad.

Save yourself the money and skip to making healthful, long-term dietary changes instead.

How not to lose muscle while burning fat?

Most people want to know how to build bigger muscles, while burning a large amount of fat at the same time. In fact, some say you can definitely do both at the same time where others deny otherwise.

This has been debated for quite some time now. Well, the answer to this question is yes and no and depends.

You see, you can build bigger muscles and burn fat at the same time. However, if you are using a fat loss exercise workout routine and also at the same time going through a fat loss diet, you will not be able to build a lot of muscles.

You will also burn more fats during your routines if your body possesses more muscles. Well, it is a common impression that more muscles will cause a person to look big and bulky, but this is not always the case.

Bodybuilders are known to have a small amount of body fat while having a huge amount of muscles.

The reason why body builders are able to burn fat and muscles because they do it in phases. It is called periodization in the muscle building world. When body builders build muscles, their diet differs drastically from their exercise routines compared to when they are in the phase of losing fats. These body builders will build mass muscles for several months by segmenting different body part workout routines, as well as lifting heavy weight with low repetitions. It is only that they will change their diet completely from one of building muscle to one which is trying to lose fat. If you have the time, energy and dedication, you may work towards that time of routine, hence, eventually becoming a body builder yourself. But if you just a novice exerciser who just wishes to burn fat and build muscles which are just nice, you can choose a routine and diet which you can burn fat and at the same time, burn a small amount of muscle.

A great way you can approach this to undergo cardio training combined with total body strength training. You see when you perform total body strength training, this will help you to increase your metabolism rate to help you to burn the unwanted fats. When combined with the right type of cardio training, you are on the pathway to successfully burn fats and building bigger muscles at the same time.

Not to forget, your diet will affect your capability to burn fat and muscle too. Consuming quality protein, healthy fats, and complex carbohydrate in a small meal scale 4 - 6 times a day will help you burn more fats because your blood sugar is more constant to help in controlling your appetite.

Tips to build muscle and burn fat

The goal of many body builders is to gain muscles while burning fats. In order to gain muscles, the body needs food and reduction of extraneous activities. While burning fats the body needs much few calories and lots of more tedious cardiovascular exercises. If one wants to embark on a mutual compromise between bulking and cutting typically would result to a compromise outcome. Possibly burning fats without muscle gain or vice versa.

With the advancement of knowledge and understanding the various system of human body and its function, one can apply correct exercise and nutritional intake to better enable one to achieve the goal of increasing muscle mass and losing fat simultaneously.

Here are tips on how to build muscle and burn fats:

1. Engage in cardiovascular exercise

Cardiovascular exercises should be done 3-6 days alternated between longer, slow duration cardio and fast cardio exercise. Walking on a slightly inclined treadmill for 45 minutes is an ideal form of the longer duration cardiovascular exercise, which should be performed on weight training days up to 3x a week. Sprinting outdoors, on a treadmill and/or cycling is an ideal form of fast cardiovascular exercise, which should be done on weight training off days 2-3 times per week.

2. Do weight training

The actual weight training exercises is as important as the timing. It is important to do this exercise in the late afternoon and early evening to allow one to burn fat throughout the day. It is at this time when one will be eating a lower calorie and low carbohydrates diet. Doing exercise too early in the day would halt fat burning for the rest of the day. It should be early in the evening to allow 6 hours interval between weight training session and bedtime. During sleep is the time to drive protein synthesis and replenish glycogen stores. The weight training should be done 3 times a week on alternate days. Each session should consist of heavy basic compound movements with some overlap. Example to it would be chest and back focus on Monday, leg focus on Wednesday, shoulders and arms focus on Friday. All the exercises should be hard, heavy, intense, and cover the entire body.

3. Do a two separate phase of diet.

The diet should be done in two separate phases, the low calorie low carbohydrate portion and the high calorie and high carbohydrate portion. The guidelines would be, all days on weight training off days and half day on weight training days, one should have low calorie diet. Calorie intake of 10-12 times the body weight, consisting of 50% protein, 30 % fat and 20% carbohydrates.

During weight training days, one should have high calorie, high carbohydrate diet.

Calorie intake should be 10-12 times the body weight, consisting of 20% protein, 5% fats and 75% carbohydrates. The meal should be consumed in a span of 6-8 hours.

On maintenance phase, calorie intake should be 15 times the body weight, consisting of 50% protein, 30% fat and 20 % carbohydrates.

The weight training and dieting phase do not only burn fats but also put the body to a glycogen-depleted state that heightens insulin sensitivity. By doing so, the body is ready to suck up on all the nutrients delivered during the short-term carbohydrate overfeed. There will be an increase in levels of insulin as the body responds to this overfeeding. Studies have shown that there will be a very small effect on conversion of carbohydrate to fats during massive short-term carbohydrate overfeeding.

4. Take supplements

Taking supplements can help in achieving the required nutritional value to build muscles and reduce fats.

There are several ways to achieve muscle bulk at the same time losing weight. The right combination and timing of diet and exercise is the key. So if one is dreaming to gain muscle and shed off those fats, follow the four tips mentioned above.

How to build a diet that works

It is simply amazing how fast the body will revert to the way it was designed to look when we enact proper nutrition and strength building exercise upon it. In order for a diet to work fast, people must take both halves of the program seriously. In fact, there are countless cases where a 'morbidly obese' person completely changes their diet and starts to do exercises designed to increase muscle mass, resulting in amazing success.

These people, almost without fail, lose the greatest percentage of fat in the first month of the program. Anyone who watches the program, the Biggest Loser, has seen the huge results that the committed contestants achieve in the first three or four weeks of the show.

The body WANTS to be perfect. It is designed to be a lean, tough, survival-driven machine and not a sedentary, fat-storing body.

The body WILL store fat because, according to theorists, human ancestors had to go long periods of time without meat or bountiful food supplies. So, the body learned to store a little for those long migrations and periods of time.

The unfortunate side effect of that human genetic disposition is that now people can choose to eat constantly or get into a rut of snacking constantly. The kinds of diets that work the fastest or those that are primarily built on high-quality, lean protein, good carbohydrates, and healthy fats and oils. Of course, with any recommended diet, drinking more water will do wonders to boost the metabolism and speed up the journey to the desired results.

Eating 5 or 6 smaller meals a day and hitting a specific calorie count per day, while adding strength and muscle building exercise will show the results of our labor within weeks. Normally, a person's face will look noticeably thinner within 5 to 7 days. The double chin seems to be where the body likes to take its stored energy first, visibly speaking.

People looking for diets that work fast and who have a realistic sense of how much work they need to get to their ideal weight are usually people looking to just drop a few extra pounds so they can fit into a dress or swimsuit by the next week or two. For people who need to lose 30 lbs. or more, fast does not mean one or two weeks. Considering that the body of work that must be completed is greater for someone who has not taken in the right foods or has not stuck to an exercise program in years than for someone who has just slacked off for the past couple of weeks.

So, in the case of needing to burn more fat, fast certainly will not equal easy. In order to show real gains within two or three weeks, eating must be taken to a level of perfection and exercise must be done six times per week.

This is not news to anyone, but before putting new kinds of stress on your body, talk to a doctor and get the okay to do so. Taking on a workout program like Shaun T's Insanity or P90X after 10 years of bodily abuse by diet, smoking, and laziness could do damage in the short-term. Some people will need to warm up with lighter workouts, but the diet still must be absolutely perfect if the gains they are looking for are to be accomplished in a relatively short period of time. In the end, the diets that work the fastest are the ones that only allow the three healthy food pillars mentioned above, involve muscle-building exercise, and increase the amount of water the person drinks.

You have been bombarded lately by so many ads online or in TV trying to suggest the only diets that work for you. Yet, none of these guaranteed weight loss plans did not produce any result or you have lost couple pounds, but not for long.

Now you sitting back behind your computer trying to look for another fad diets that will give you the answer you've been searching for: What are the diets that work?

To be very honest with you is that the diets that are promoted are all garbage. Yes. Garbage. None of those fad diet do not work. It might start making sense to you why you could not lose weight. Also you should know that all those diets are the cause of you Yo-Yo Dieting, losing fat and gaining more in couple of weeks, being cranky and stressful etc.

As hard as it is to believe diets are nothing else that the way you eat! So if you are going to McDonnald every day, you are probably on McBurger diet. If you go to your nearest Pizza shop, you are on a pizza diet. Those are not diets that will help you to lose fat and reveal your six-pack.

Then you have diets that have all components and food groups like chicken, beans and rice. Or sweet potato with broccoli and char-coal grilled chicken breast.

What these diets contain is protein (needed to build muscles), carbohydrates (needed to feed your brain and give you source of energy) and vegetables (filled with nutrients, minerals and fiber to feed every cell of your body and help you digest better).

And at last you have the above mentioned diets that scream at you when watching TV, listening the radio or browsing online search engines. Most of them will make you lose weight, but it won't be fat loss but major muscle loss. You really can't afford to lose muscles. Because what you will gain back will be more fat. You will completely change your body composition and that is what will make it much harder to lose fat in the future.

So stop chasing those diets that will remove either proteins, carbs or fibers out of your diet. Your perfect diets that work for you should have all food groups and therefore basic building blocks for body. Nothing more, nothing less.

Many people don't get a clear idea of how to choose the diet that works for them. This is usually because they feel misled or do not clearly understand the complicated language used in diet books. To make things simpler, let's set categories of lifestyles where you could recognize your way of living so that you start losing pounds now.

Are you someone who performs strenuous jobs daily and stay in the sun? If yes, it is important to know that a healthy diet is different for you too. People who make a lot of effort spend calories while at work. A diet with a higher rate of energy in the form of fats, protein and carbohydrates is acceptable in this case, however, it is also very important to consume water plentifully. Fruits and vegetables are also important.

Are you the type of person who does his/her work sitting? The form of energy you will be using in that case will surely also make you feel as tired too. This is because you need some fresh air. It is very important to take plenty of fruits and vegetables in this case as they are essential to remedy your tired nerves. Fats should really be avoided and protein foods should be taken in small quantities only.

Are you recovering from a long sickness or did you have an accident and got your bones broken? When something is wrong in your body, your body cells and tissues usually get affected and make you feel ill. You get feverish or rashes because your body had been undergoing a war with germs. This may require you to do a lot of cleaning up and replacing the dead cells. For this, food rich in protein and vitamins and minerals are very important. If you have fractures, it does not really mean you're sick. But food rich in calcium is important to build your bones anew!

So how do you find diets that work?

Simply these diets should not tell you to eat less and starve yourselves. They should not tell you to eat less carbs, no protein, no vegetables. They can't drastically lower your daily calorie intake and they should not sell you on some miracle pills and do nothing.

Only you can choose what diet is best for you. You just need to get more educated about foods, exercise and stress reduction. Remember, your diet is the one you feel fantastic about. No chores or drudgery there. Then you know that you have found diets that work for you.

There are people in the world today who want to have an attractive look as well as nice figure. These people spend a fortune on diets that can help them lose weight. There are a lot of sites that can suggest meals or diets that "work" when one wants to lose weight. But many of these sites are best left avoided since the diet programs they suggest are rather ambiguous and could even jeopardize your plans to shed that excess weight you have. A recent study has shown that Americans are spending more or less $70 billion dollars a year when it comes to dieting and losing weight and the figure goes up annually.

Real diets that work when it comes to losing weight and having an attractive figure include those espoused by professionals such as dietitians, doctors and nutritionists among others. In making preparations for charting a diet, elements like age, preference in food, gender, work and so forth are to be considered. The diets being planned for the chart can be varied for every meal. For example, you can have some fruit as a snack while you can have some vegetables along with pasta for lunch, as these have low levels of fat. The same can be said for your breakfast as well as the dinner you'll be having. Foods such as fruits and vegetables are a very sustainable source of energy. In time, you can develop a reduced liking to something like fast food.

In case you want to build up your muscle mass, there are also diets that work on that. What you need to do so is to have high protein meals. These include meat such as chicken, beef and turkey, fish as well as free-range eggs. Foods having high protein content increase the feeling of being "full" and, in time also lower your craving to overeat.

In addition to the ones mentioned, you should also seek professional advice since this can help you plan balanced diets in more detail in addition to helping you get motivated. These professionals know how to prepare diets that work depending on what sort of activities you do and what sort of food you like.

Diets that work are prepared with losing weight as well as maintaining a body that's fit as well as healthy. What's vital to a diet that succeeds is in having an air of positivity when it comes to living life as well as the conviction to change the way you eat.

An easy diet plan

Are you tired and want to lose those unwanted inches and pounds that you have gained over the last couple of years. All because you were feeling old, unattractive and not that interested in anything at all. Well let me put your mind to rest, because you are not alone. There are hundreds of people online right now that feel like you do, and doing the same thing you are. Their looking to find a diet that will work and provide all the information they need to make an informative decision.

There are a number of diets that work well, very well. You might have seen the show, "The Biggest Loser" on TV. That Diet or Weight Loss Plan works very, very well. People lose and incredible amount of weight each week. Double digit weight losses are very common for most of the contestants. That would be unhealthy for most but those contestants are closely monitored and fed special diets. Most important is they have so much excess water and fat build up that it is healthier for them to get rid of it at that rate. They are put on a exercise program that pushes them to vomit and tears.

Most of us can't afford or don't have the luxury of having that much time to go to a health resort for that kind of weight loss program. That's too bad because most of us need to be educated on the importance of proper nutrition and good fitness.

The contestants on the biggest loser have that advantage. They are fully examined and are sat down at told there realistic age of their body. They are shown what their organs look like compared to a normal organ. They are shown why they are going to die at a much earlier age than a normal life span. That gives them a good start on the mindset needed to go through a serious weight loss plan and then to continue to diet. The other half of the mindset is they are asked to write down all the reasons they want to get healthy and live a long life. Once a person has good reasons to live longer and is shown the reasons why that won't happen the mindset is in place. That is an important part to a long lasting lifestyle change.

Not every diet works for everybody. In fact, it is not always the diet that does not work. Certain diets work differently for different people. Diets that work for one may not work for another. Everyone is different, and all the pills, powders, liquids and systems, programs and plans all work differently, too. Some pills will make you very shaky. This is due to the caffeine in them. The weight only comes off when you are putting in the effort. If you are not trying or you are just taking the pills and hoping for the best. No, of course it is not going to work, you cannot lose five pounds in five days without trying. There is a lot of work that has to take place in order to lose weight.

Eating healthy food and excise is a much better way to lose weight, this is how the revolutionary diet plan, Strip That Fat fits into your life. I consider this a true diet plan, you eat real food 4 - 5 times a day, so you are not starving yourself. And with this diet plan you get what is called the Strip That Fat Diet Generator software which you enter into the generator, the foods you like to eat, then it sets up a diet plan that you follow. When you what to make changes within your diet plan just enter into the diet generator what you want and again it will create another plan for you. It also prints a shopping list to help make it easier to get what you need, in order to follow your diet plan.

It also comes with a guide that explains everything you need to know about dieting, like what works and why, what does not work and the reasons why they don't. The complete Strip That Fat Diet Plan and Generator and all the information you could possible want to assist you along the way to your weight loss goal.

There must be some form of exercise in order to lose that unwanted fat. A brisk walk every day is a great way to start, increasing your heart rate to the fat burning zone for at least 15 minutes to start. Then as you get comfortable with that you can start to build 20, 30 minutes, increasing slowly. You can strip those unwanted ponds and inches right off in no time at all.

There are very few diets or weight loss plans that make it simple by teaching proper nutrition without making drastic lifestyle changes. Also teach simple exercises that slowly tone your body instead of drastic lifestyle changes of daily vigorous workouts. If you try to change your lifestyle too quickly in too many different ways it usually will fail. That is what studies show. A plan that "Works" is one that you can live with for life. That is a good healthy weight loss plan or diet that works.

So if you're looking for one that works, do some research and read what the plans intentions are. See if it teaches you all about nutrition and lets you eat the foods you like to eat. See if it is something you can live with for long term, not just short term. Why pay a lot of money for something that is not going to last long? Why suffer for a short term loss of weight? If you learn how to lose weight properly it isn't real difficult. Weight goes on one pound at a time over a long period of time and that is how it should come off.

If your definition of "works" is just lose a few pounds then quit and gain it back then start all over again, take your pick of plans, they all "Work".

How to Improve your Energy-Boosting Effect (EBE)

We all lead such hectic lives that being constantly tired or lacking energy can seem almost normal for many people. Just getting by can take up most of our energy, leaving little left to use to work towards our goals or building our ideal life.

It seems that most successful people have high energy levels. There may be exceptions, but I think it's fair to say that there's probably not that many examples of people who are constantly tired or exhausted, or burned out, achieving and sustaining high levels of success.

So what can we do to increase our energy levels?

Getting enough sleep, relaxing and taking time off when you don't work at all, are the most obvious essentials to maintaining energy levels.

It will also help if we understand the different types of energy we use in our lives. There is more than one type of energy. The main types of energy are physical, emotional and mental. Although these are distinctly different, they are closely related and interdependent.

Physical Energy

Physical energy is the most basic type of energy. This is the energy that's used in manual labour. People who are involved in this kind of work usually need to eat substantial quantities of food just to sustain themselves. In many cases, at the end of each day they will have little energy left over for anything more than relaxing and sleeping so they can rebuild their strength in preparation for the next day. This is the situation for much of the world's population, particularly in developing countries.

Fortunately, due to automation, labour saving inventions, computers etc many of us no longer have to work as hard physically as previous generations did. More people than ever are employed in knowledge based roles requiring little or no physical effort.

Emotional Energy

Emotional energy is the energy that allows us to experience happiness, joy, love, excitement and many other emotions, both good and bad. This is the energy that gives us our enthusiasm and our love of life, and allows us to have fun. Many of our actions are driven, in varying degrees, by our emotional energy. Our emotions can have a great impact on our overall energy levels.

When you are with friends and loved ones and are happy, excited or having fun, you will usually find that you have plenty you energy and feel great. This type of interaction with others not only boosts energy levels, but is good for overall health and resistance to illness.

Unsurprisingly, negative emotions have the opposite effect. If you are feeling angry, upset, depressed, frustrated or stressed, for example, you'll find your energy levels depleted and your resistance weak. If you keep feeling this way for extended periods, you'll eventually burn out altogether. If you can maximise positive emotions and maintain an overall optimistic outlook you'll find that you have more energy that you can put to good use in other areas of your life.

Mental Energy

The other type of energy is mental energy. As many of us now work in knowledge based roles, we use a lot of this type of energy on a daily basis. This is the energy of creativity, decision making, writing, reading, learning new information and much more. Most of us now rely on our mental energy to survive.

How effectively we use our mental energy will ultimately decide how successful we are in our lives. It is our mental energy, through our thought processes, that determines our values and goals and the actions we take, which ultimately determine what we make of our lives.

How well we maximise the use of our mental energy and powers will be a major factor determining how successful and happy our lives turn out.

Negative Energy

One common setback to success is burning up energy in destructive ways. Although most of us don't now engage in much hard physical work, many of us waste huge amounts of emotional energy. This can take many forms. It could be something a common as having a generally negative outlook on life. There are many other examples, such as being over sensitive or easily upset, or being prone to emotional outbursts of anger or even violence.

Negative emotions can massively drain energy levels, in fact a five minute outburst of anger uses about as much energy as eight hours of mental work.

Being at your best mentally depends on being at your best emotionally. Keeping calm, not letting things bother you, and maintaining a positive mental outlook can make a huge difference to your emotional state, which will boost your mental and physical energy. So will ensuring you get enough sleep, taking time to relax and taking regular breaks where you forget your work altogether. These can be the critical difference between being always tired, highly stressed or constantly on edge, and enjoying a successful, rewarding and happy life.

How to increase your energy levels

Do you feel you are performing at your best? Do you spring out of bed in the morning, excited and ready for the opportunities your day presents? Imagine for a moment you are the proud owner of a champion, thorough bred horse worth in excess of one million dollars.

As the owner of this prized purebred, would you let him stay up half the night, drink coffee and booze, smoke cigarettes and eat junk food? What about your $10 dog? Your $5 cat?

You see, most people treat their own bodies with less care than they would treat a $5 cat. If you did own a horse worth one million dollars, you would hire a nutritionist to make sure his diet was exactly right, you would also ensure he was getting his regular massages and spine alignment treatments; the best supplementation; you would have the best trainer in the country; an air-conditioned barn in the summer time, a steam-heated one in the winter time a million dollar investment. And here you have this BILLION dollar body.

When Was Your Last 100,000km Service?

The problem is that we expect our body will just do what it is supposed to do no matter what kind of treatment it receives. We often take better care of our car ensuring it gets regular service, appropriate maintenance and oil changes in the necessary intervals, but when it comes to our own bodies, the service is usually below par.

Our bodies have amazing coping, self-correcting mechanisms. It is able to handle, quite literally, long-term abuse, without much complaint for long periods. It waits patiently to be treated well with only slow and gradual decline in health and vitality, until the day it decides: That's it, I've had enough!--only then we start paying attention.

The First Sign, Help Is Needed!

The first aspect of our health that starts to signal a need for 'help' relates to our general wellbeing and vitality: Our energy levels. We often misinterpret the body's needs or simply ignore them--what the body really is asking for when it lacks energy is for us to take care: sleep more, eat well, exercise, re-hydrate. But instead of that we end up giving it lots of coffee, energy drinks, sugar and telling ourselves to 'snap out of it' as we go on abusing it. That is not a smart long-term strategy. In fact, it only leads to one thing: Disease.

How Do I Make It All Better?

The solution is to STOP and go back to basics. However, before you change anything it is vital to assess where you are at and where you would like to be. In my practice we have some fancy machines to do that, we also take our patients through very comprehensive and detailed assessments to ensure we are both clear about the starting point (a baseline is paramount), however one of the tools we use which is available to you right now is a simple question:--What are you energy levels on a scale of 0-10 10=excellent)? Once you have the answer to this question you can start implementing the following suggestions to substantially increase your energy levels. In fact, a 300% energy increase is very realistic. When a person is operating at 2/10 and for the time, that is their 100%, it doesn't take long, when applying the tips below to increase levels to a generous and vibrant 8/10. Keep going and you will ACE it!

Practical Steps For Energy Maximization

Once you know where you are at, you can measure your progress as you go along. Here are 7 tips that will transform your energy levels and vitality within one week of diligent application. The catch is that you need to keep your practice up for at least 28 days to see the full benefit of your new investment in yourself.

1. Clean Up Your Diet

Let go of all junk. Base your meals on fresh, organic, seasonal produce (fruits and vegetables) and good quality protein (e.g. eggs, quark, chicken, beef, lamb, kangaroo, venison etc). The less unprocessed your foods the better. Avoid canned and pre-prepared meals.

2. Have Protein For Breakfast

If you could only do ONE thing on this list--this would have to be it. Eating good quality protein for breakfast is one of the only things that will ensure you do not get any energy slumps in the afternoon. So try poached or boiled eggs; fruit smoothie with quark; fruit with cottage cheese or quark; toast with sardines or (flaked) grilled salmon.

3. Eat Every 3 Hours

This will ensure your energy is leveled during the day. Ensuring your moods, focus, concentration are all optimum. This is easier than you think. Just divide up what you would normally eat in one sitting for a meal into two. Your digestive system will have an easier job and your energy levels will skyrocket.

4. What To Drink And What Not To Drink?

When cells become dehydrated, they don't perform the metabolic processed necessary to ensure proper detoxification and optimum energy. So ensuring you have a large 2L bottle with you or a jug on your desk--knowing that by the end of the day the whole thing needs to be finished will be your best way forward. Also ensure your have a good quality water filter for this purpose; toxins found in unfiltered or poorly filtered water will damage your health. You want to make sure your filter is as fine as 1 micron or more.

In addition, be sure to avoid (or at least drastically cut down on the consumption of) coffee and alcohol, as well as sugary and energy drinks including undiluted fruit juices. These substances dramatically disturb your blood sugar levels and energy balance. Coffee and alcohol are also very dehydrating, also depleting the body of essential nutrients necessary to ensure optimum energy.

5. Get Enough And Quality Sleep

If your body is not resting sufficiently at night--no matter what you do during the day, your energy levels will not improve. Start by planning your life around getting enough sleep, not the other way around. Budget for 7-9 hours of sleep time each night. If you are having problems, sleeping you will see that by implementing all the previous suggestions this should improve. Alternatively, seek help; there are many effective natural tools you can implement for a better night's sleep.

6. Exercise & Nutritional support

Being active is the best way to balance your blood sugar levels. Also when you exercise your body releases endorphins which are feel good chemicals that also boost your energy levels. There are so many benefits to exercise, if you are not doing it, you are missing out! Aim to do something for at least 40 minutes, no less 4 days per week. Build up to this slowly if necessary--but just get out there!

7. Spinal Alignment & Nutritional Support

It is all very well to want to build a house, but if you are missing key building materials, it is not going to happen--no matter how much you want it. This is the role of nutrients in the body. Unfortunately when the body becomes depleted, diet alone is not sufficient to correct the problem. Each individual has different requirement and an assessment of your needs, as well as what other supplements or medicines you are currently taking is really important before embarking on any new supplementation. Resolving depleted or deficient states in your body can make a world of difference to your energy levels!

Another key aspect of energy is spinal your spine health and alignment--this also hinges on appropriate nutritional markers, however ensuring proper blood flow to tissues, and key body parts such as the brain is essential for energy and for this you just cannot go passed a good chiropractor or osteopath.

Keep these up and your billion dollar asset will reward you with bountiful energy, remarkable vitality and robust wellbeing. What more could you want?

Delicious Sirtfood Diet Recipes

The Sirtfood Juice

A good way to start is with The Sirtfood Juice – so we've thrown in the recipe for this to start you off as a bonus extra. The book advises drinking 3 juices and adding 1 meal for the first 3 days, then 2 juices, 2 meals for the next 4.Sirtfood Green Juice (serves 1)

Ingredients:

- 2 large handfuls (75g) kale
- a large handful (30g) rocket
- a very small handful (5g) flat-leaf parsley
- a very small handful (5g) lovage leaves (optional)
- 2–3 large stalks (150g) green celery, including its leaves
- ½ medium green apple
- juice of ½ lemon
- ½ level tsp matcha green tea

Instructions:

Mix the greens (kale, rocket, parsley and lovage, if using) together, then juice them. We find juicers can really differ in their efficiency at juicing leafy vegetables and you may need to re-juice the remnants before moving on to the other ingredients. The goal is to end up with about 50ml of juice from the greens.

Now juice the celery and apple. You can peel the lemon and put it through the juicer as well, but we find it much easier to simply squeeze the lemon by hand into the juice. By this stage, you should have around 250ml of juice in total, perhaps slightly more. It is only when the juice is made and ready to serve that you add the matcha green tea.

Pour a small amount of the juice into a glass, then add the matcha and stir vigorously with a fork or teaspoon. We only use matcha in the first two drinks of the day as it contains moderate amounts of caffeine (the same content as a normal cup of tea). For people not used to it, it may keep them awake if drunk late. Once the matcha is dissolved add the remainder of the juice.

Give it a final stir, then your juice is ready to drink. Feel free to top up with plain water, according to taste.

Sirt Muesli (serves 1)

If you want to make this in bulk or prepare it the night before, simply combine the dry ingredients and store it in an airtight container. All you need to do the next day is add the strawberries and yoghurt and it's good to go.

Ingredients:

- 20g buckwheat flakes
- 10g buckwheat puffs
- 15g coconut flakes or desiccated coconut
- 40g Medjool dates, pitted and chopped
- 15g walnuts, chopped
- 10g cocoa nibs

- 100g strawberries, hulled and chopped

- 100g plain Greek yoghurt (or vegan alternative, such as soya or coconut yoghurt)

Instructions:

Mix all of the above ingredients together (leave out the strawberries and yoghurt if not serving straight away).

Aromatic chicken breast with kale and red onions and a tomato and chilli salsa (serves 1)

Ingredients:

- 120g skinless, boneless chicken breast

- 2 tsp ground turmeric

- juice of ¼ lemon

- 1 tbsp extra virgin olive oil

- 50g kale, chopped

- 20g red onion, sliced

- 1 tsp chopped fresh ginger

- 50g buckwheat

- For the salsa

- 130g tomato (about 1)

- 1 bird's eye chilli, finely chopped

- 1 tbsp capers, finely chopped

- 5g parsley, finely chopped

- Juice of ¼ lemon

Instructions:

To make the salsa, remove the eye from the tomato and chop it very finely, taking care to keep as much of the liquid as possible. Mix with the chilli, capers, parsley and lemon juice. You could put everything in a blender but the end result is a little different.

Heat the oven to 220°C/gas 7. Marinate the chicken breast in 1 teaspoon of the turmeric, the lemon juice and a little oil. Leave for 5–10 minutes.Heat an ovenproof frying pan until hot, then add the marinated chicken and cook for a minute or so on each side, until pale golden, then transfer to the oven (place on a baking tray if your pan isn't ovenproof) for 8–10 minutes or until cooked through. Remove from the oven, cover with foil and leave to rest for 5 minutes before serving.

Meanwhile, cook the kale in a steamer for 5 minutes. Fry the red onions and the ginger in a little oil, until soft but not coloured, then add the cooked kale and fry for another minute.Cook the buckwheat according to the packet instructions with the remaining teaspoon of turmeric. Serve alongside the chicken, vegetables and salsa.

Sirtfood bites (makes 15-20 bites)

Ingredients:

- 120g walnuts
- 30g dark chocolate (85 per cent cocoa solids), broken into pieces; or cocoa nibs
- 250g Medjool dates, pitted
- 1 tbsp cocoa powder
- 1 tbsp ground turmeric
- 1 tbsp extra virgin olive oil
- the scraped seeds of 1 vanilla pod or 1 tsp vanilla extract
- 1–2 tbsp water

Instructions:

Place the walnuts and chocolate in a food processor and process until you have a fine powder.

Add all the other ingredients except the water and blend until the mixture forms a ball. You may or may not have to add the water depending on the consistency of the mixture – you don't want it to be too sticky.

Using your hands, form the mixture into bite-sized balls and refrigerate in an airtight container for at least 1 hour before eating them. You could roll some of the balls in some more cocoa or desiccated coconut to achieve a different finish if you like. They will keep for up to 1 week in your fridge.

Asian king prawn stir-fry with buckwheat noodles (serves 1)

Ingredients:

- 150g shelled raw king prawns, deveined
- 2 tsp tamari (you can use soy sauce if you are not avoiding gluten)
- 2 tsp extra virgin olive oil
- 75g soba (buckwheat noodles)
- 1 garlic clove, finely chopped
- 1 bird's eye chilli, finely chopped
- 1 tsp finely chopped fresh ginger
- 20g red onions, sliced
- 40g celery, trimmed and sliced
- 75g green beans, chopped
- 50g kale, roughly chopped
- 100ml chicken stock
- 5g lovage or celery leaves

Instructions:

Heat a frying pan over a high heat, then cook the prawns in 1 teaspoon of the tamari and 1 teaspoon of the oil for 2–3 minutes. Transfer the prawns to a plate. Wipe the pan out with kitchen paper, as you're going to use it again.

Cook the noodles in boiling water for 5–8 minutes or as directed on the packet. Drain and set aside. Meanwhile, fry the garlic, chilli and ginger, red onion, celery, beans and kale in the remaining oil over a medium–high heat for 2–3 minutes. Add the stock and bring to the boil, then simmer for a minute or two, until the vegetables are cooked but still crunchy.

Add the prawns, noodles and lovage/celery leaves to the pan, bring back to the boil then remove from the heat and serve.

Strawberry buckwheat tabouleh

Ingredients:

- 50g buckwheat
- 1 tbsp ground turmeric
- 80g avocado
- 65g tomato
- 20g red onion
- 25g Medjool dates, pitted
- 1 tbsp capers
- 30g parsley
- 100g strawberries, hulled
- 1 tbsp extra virgin olive oil
- juce of ½ lemon
- 30g rocket

Instructions:

Cook the buckwheat with the turmeric according to the packet instructions. Drain and keep to one side to cool.

Finely chop the avocado, tomato, red onion, dates, capers and parsley and mix with the cool buckwheat. Slice the strawberries and gently mix into the salad with the oil and lemon juice. Serve on a bed of rocket.

KETO DIET FOR WOMEN OVER 50

Beginners Guide to Start Living a Happy & Healthy Life, Losing Weight Fast and Naturally

|May 2021 Edition|

Introduction

What's keto?

Keto is a diet program that needs cutting carbohydrates and raising carbs with the objective of helping your body burn its fat stores better.

Studies have shown this ketogenic diets are valuable for total health and slimming down. Notably, ketogenic diets also have helped particular people shed unwanted body weight with no extreme cravings which are typical of different diets.

It has also been discovered that a few individuals with type two diabetes may use keto for a means to control their own symptoms.

Why you ought to read this book

You need to read this publication since it includes how ketogenic diet works, to understand the type of food you need to eat and the kinds of food that you should avoid

How ketogenic diets function

Ketones are at the middle of the ketogenic diet plan.

Your entire body produces ketones, a gas molecule, even as an alternate energy source once the body is running low on blood glucose.

Producing ketones happens when you lose carbohydrate consumption and eat only the perfect quantity of protein.

When you are ingesting keto beneficial foods, so your liver may move body fat into ketones, which get used as a power source from the physique.

After the body is employing fat for a power supply, you are in ketosis.

This permits the body to boost its fat burning drastically in some instances, which aids in lowering pockets of undesirable fat.

Not only does this procedure of fat burning assist you get rid of weight, but in addition, it can ward off cravings and protect against energy crashes through the day.

What foods are keto-approved?

While it's easy to state that the keto diet is packed with fat and saturated in carbohydrates, it always looks somewhat more complex when you are at the grocery store aisle.

Here's a listing of meals on keto for women over 50. **What foods to eat keto:**

- **meat:** search for unprocessed meats since they have fewer (or no) added carbohydrates
- **fish and fish:** prevent breaded fish for the additional carbohydrates
- **eggs:** ready yet you like best
- **vegetables:** individuals who grow over the floor
- **dairy:** select for high fat milk; low-carb options frequently have additional sugar
- **nuts:** great supply of fat, however be careful to not overeat
- **berries:** in moderation

What foods not to eat keto

- **sugar:** the most important thing to cut
- **fruit:** some small fruit is okay, but also considerably increases sugar to a diet
- **beer/alcohol:** a lot of carbohydrates and sugars
- **starches:** white bread, rice, potatoes, pasta

How to establish the advantages of this publication

In this book, you will locate the excellent advantages of both keto diet and the way that it can help you

Greatest weight loss workouts for girls

Weight on keto for girls over 50hile that the keto diet provides many advantages in weight loss and total wellbeing, it is always advisable to pair diet.

Our 3-day combination mother jumpstart includes all you want to receive your fitness center in equipment.

From recipe thoughts to workout programs, you will have the ability to try our fit mother training for 3 days of strength.

All our strategies are created for busy moms just like you. No crash diets, no 3-hour work outs.

Just science-backed principles which can allow you to feel the best you've in years.

Can be a keto diet great for girls over 50?

Whether or not keto is best for you depends upon on lots of variables.

Keto for ladies over 50 presuming you do not suffer from health difficulties, a ketogenic diet may

offer many advantages, particularly for weight reduction.

The most important consideration to consider is to consume a fantastic balance of veggies, lean beef, and unsalted carbohydrates.

Simply sticking to whole foods is most probably the most effective way of eating easily, mainly since it is a sustainable strategy.

It is important to be aware a lot of research suggests ketogenic diets are tough to stay with. Because of this, the very best advice is to seek out a wholesome way of eating that is right for you.

It is ok to try new items, just don't jump in head first.

What Can I Eat On a Keto Diet?

CAN EAT

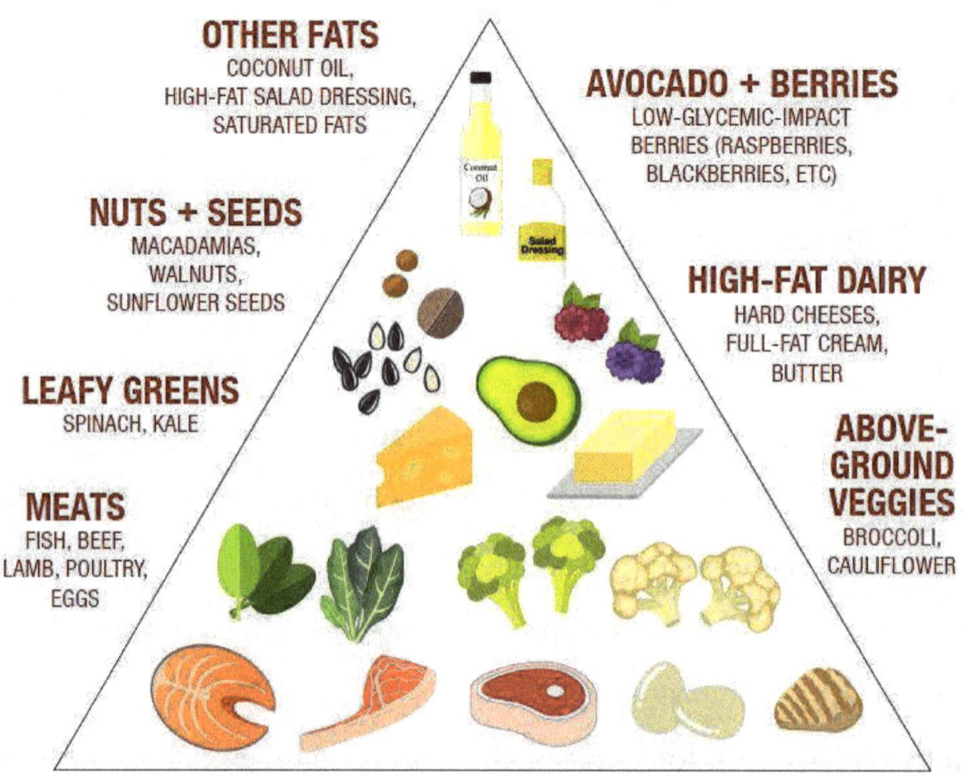

AVOID

GRAINS
WHEAT, CORN, RICE, CEREAL

SUGAR
HONEY, AGAVE, MAPLE SYRUP

FRUIT
APPLES, BANANAS, ORANGES

STARCHY ROOT VEGGIES
POTATO, YAMS

CHAPTER ONE: Body modifications following 50

Body dimensions after 50: how much could you control? Weight gain and belly fat

Take weight reduction, for instance. Women and men wind up gaining weight at a speed of one or two pounds each year between early adulthood and middle age.

Girls especially tend to obtain belly fat. Though moving through menopause is frequently regarded as an expected element of aging, study proves it doesn't lead to a woman to gain weight. An overview by the worldwide menopause society discovered that, although weight gain isn't brought on by menopause, hormonal fluctuations in this period can, however, cause more stomach fat. Environmental and lifestyle factors are mostly to blame for your weight reduction itself, scientists reasoned.

In insulin resistance, fat, liver and muscle cells don't respond normally to insulin. Consequently, liver cells don't consume glucose (blood glucose) readily from the blood vessels, a condition that may keep blood glucose levels greater than normal and also boost the chance of type two diabetes.

Metabolism changes and weight

Another variable contributing to weight reduction is a fall in metabolism, which starts to decrease on your 30s.

"metabolism is down between 10 and 15 per cent by age 50," states boling. Reduction of muscle leads primarily to a decline in metabolism, because muscle burns more calories at rest than fat loss.

"muscle reduction is among the very underrated health problems later 40 and 50," says suzette pereira, writer together with abbott nutrition, columbus, ohio, specializing in muscle building and muscle loss related to age. "thirty to 40 per cent of our entire body is muscle. Muscle loss happens gradually but hastens time."

Feeling poorer or discussing after a walk might be indications of muscle reduction, boling states. Muscle atrophy additionally relates to bones and may bring about osteoporosis as time passes.

A poll by aarp and abbott of almost 1,500 people discovered that although 73% of survey participants realize they obviously get rid of muscle using age, just 13 percent understand the significance of keeping muscle mass with age.

"it is not about stomach and biceps. "it is all about fat burning and keeping up your posture and dealing with health drawbacks." over a third of respondents reported to be hospitalized following 50 because of chronic illness; reduction of muscle and strength were one of their best recovery issues.

"your body burns off through muscle once you are sick. The expression "sarcopenia" identifies the decrease of muscle tissue linked to the aging procedure. "sarcopenia sets you at high risk of losing independence. Muscle loss is just one of the largest causes of complete functional decline in elderly adults.

Along with modifications in muscle, tendons and ligaments (which attach muscle to bone), additionally alter. As a consequence of those changes (including greater melancholy and "brittleness"), adults over 50 experience improved recovery time. Injuries like tendonitis become more prone with time. Especially, ligaments and tendons of the shoulder (rotator cuff), achilles, knees and elbows tend to become more brittle and vulnerable to damage in busy individuals over 50. From age 80 a lot of men and women lose around 50% of muscular mass.

Everything you could do: resistance training is that the golden standard to maintain strength and muscle. "and then keep in mind it is never too late to begin. Your muscles possess plasticity, meaning that they may get powerful again," she notes. Though three out of four men and women in the aarp/abbott poll said that they exercise three times weekly, they largely focused on cardio vascular, maybe not strength training. "just 24 percent said that they do strength training"

Exercise goes a long way toward lessening the seriousness and effects of several physiological changes that occur as people age. A normal exercise regimen that involves strength training retains muscles wholesome. "you do not need to attend a fitness center. Home workouts are good " attempt DVDs or check out YouTube videos from qualified coaches to make certain you're using the appropriate, secure kind.

And don't forget to include enough protein, also a building block of muscle. "we become less effective at using protein because we age," states boling, that urges 30 g of protein daily.

10 things that happen on your body to a keto diet

A lot of people are jumping on board on this particular ultra-low-carb, high fat diet for a means to shed weight fast. But apart from shedding a couple pounds, keto may have a considerable influence on your entire body --good and bad. Keep reading to discover more.

You shed weight rapidly

One of those main reasons people are interested in the keto diet would be that the guarantee of rapid weight loss. "the keto diet includes a notorious reputation for fast and competitive fat reduction.

While most significant weight loss stories come from folks on intense low-carb, low-carb diets, this isn't accurate for the keto diet plan. "it isn't a starvation diet. Quite the contrary, in reality. "to maintain as much muscle as you can while to the ketogenic diet, then make sure you nourish your body as many calories because it needs." just how many calories you need is dependent upon your age, sex, and activity level.

"the fat loss is both positive and negative. "it is inspiring and helps individuals become convinced from the diet, even though it is also mainly water weight. When the weight loss stalls, it can cause people to eliminate faith and drop off the diet program " a weight reduction plateau is 1 reason people stopped the keto diet plan. Discover that the 11 reasons the majority of people today drop from the keto diet plan.

Muscle cramps can happen

Handsome muscle male jogger sporting black practice ensemble touching his knee pain together with clasped hands, using sprain or rupture within his muscles after working out outdoors.

Those abrupt cramps on your back or leg might not be in the work outs; the keto diet is to blame. "often this is because of a scarcity of potassium and sodium within the body. "sodium is thrown out of the liver while still in ketosis. The body does not hold much in book to gas itself once this comes to pass, hence adding more to this diet plan is totally nice, and frequently encouraged, to tell the truth." here is what it is like to adhere to the keto diet plan.

Your insulin sensitivity may enhance

Doctor's hand medical latex glove assessing patient's blood sugar level with syringe pen. Glucometer on the dining table.

Without glucose and carbohydrates, your body is not as likely to go through the energy rollercoaster that eating straightforward carbs generates. "since you're not able to eat starchy or sugary foods and carbohydrates, your own body's blood glucose levels are somewhat slower to grow. "this can be beneficial to people who have blood sugar problems, or type two diabetes, since it will help to raise insulin sensitivity" do not go in the keto diet blind. Read the following 15 things you want to understand prior to beginning the keto diet plan.

Your breath may odor

As your body adjusts to the dearth of sugar for fuel, so it starts to burn off the carbohydrates which were stored as glycogen in your liver, and then the fat surrounding your own organs. This generates ketones, which the human body and mind usage for fuel. "when your system gets entered into ketosis, you may notice something referred to as'acetone breath,'" weidner states.

"this occurs because if you are in ketosis, the body generates a bigger quantity of

acetone."

Actually, 1 way to quantify if you are in ketosis or is to utilize a breath test which will assess the acetone present on your breath, then weidner adds.

"[ketosis] may turned into a smelly proposal you will quickly detect," says wes shoemaker, sponsor of this youtube station highfalutin' low carb. "the acetone is removed from the body because we breathe, developing a metallic flavor and odor at the mouth area," he states.

Shoemaker adds that some keto eaters think about that the metallic flavor a fantastic sign, signs that the human body has entered ketosis and is presently burning fat--and ketones--to get fuel.

Your energy levels may stabilize, actually raise

"after your system is keto-adapted--that may take anywhere from six to 12 months -- energy levels start to stabilize. "contrary to other diets where you can experience energy spikes because of carbohydrate intake, the keto diet also gives a steady amount of energy"

"as the human body enters a state of ketosis, it gets quite resourceful in burning off fat for energy, in addition to turning fat into ketones in the liver which helps to provide energy to the mind," state the naughty nutritionists. "another theory suggests that since you provide up highly- processed, sugary foods and consume more whole foods that are essential to a keto diet your system finds out more energy with an increase in nutrients." check out why keto is really on its way to becoming one of the very popular diets to attempt.

Inflammation may be reduced

Inflammation, especially chronic inflammation, which increases your risk for many different conditions. These include cardiovascular disease, cancer, diabetes, and gut disorders. "the ketogenic diet reduces inflammation during all elements of the body. "the diet was proven to boost arthritis, irritable bowel syndrome and crohn's disease, eczema, and also be protective of the mind " and that is merely one of those 10 unforeseen health advantages of this keto diet.

You will develop a rash in the human body

"keto rash" is really a less-well-known keto-related side impact, but it sometimes happens. "while uncommon, this might be a indication of vitamin deficiency that some folks experience when beginning keto," weidner says. The rash appears as raised, red skin lesions. They may also be brown or pink. It could be uncomfortable and itchy, however, the keto rash isn't dangerous.

"people who experience this ought to widen the kinds of foods they're eating and have a multivitamin," weidner says. If the illness continues, she also adds,"check in with a physician." your physician can immediately diagnose the rash. Do not overlook these 13 things physicians would like you to understand more about the keto diet plan.

You will see modifications to your pee

You will urinate more often, and the urine could differ. "people frequently report fluctuations in the colour, odor, and consistency of the urine, in addition to urinating more often. "this is a product of the keeping less water than normal and also excreting ketones, among other items."

"when your system isn't utilizing any sugar in the bloodstream to get fuel, it divides into the liver in which the liver also stores carbs in the kind of glycogen, combined with 3 times the fat in water," in accordance with your naughty nutritionists. "since the human body burns its glycogen stores, in addition, it releases that water."

You will experience stomach troubles
Building a big dietary modification may cause some stomach problems, a healthful food delivery support. "both nausea and constipation can happen."

"constipation is a frequently-reported symptom of keto converts," shoemaker says. "drastically cutting carbs ingestion may also mean radically cutting fiber consumption -- but it does not need to."

Sure, you can not eat grains or beans over the keto dietbut you are able to load up on lots of leafy greens (kale is good) and non-starchy vegetables to boost your fiber consumption. Including lettuce, lettuce, and avocado.

"after a new ketogenic dieter adjusts for the new method of eating, they frequently see they are eating more vegetables and drinking much more water than they did on their own typical diet plan," shoemaker adds. In case you have diarrhea, then try these home remedies for nausea.

The way the body changes after 50

As we age, we now gain wisdom and expertise. We hope we really do. But our bodies finally begin showing signs of aging as muscular function, recovery capability and blood circulation begin slowing down. Then there is also the inescapable "wear-and-tear" which takes its toll on everybody at a specific age.

The way we dwelt when we were younger (and the way we decide to live today) in addition to our genetic inheritance equally have a significant impact on how healthy we are if we cross the line to our fifties.

However, it is not all lousy news: clinical investigation is making significant strides in treating age-related ailments. And great self-care and preventive steps go a very long way to lessening the effects of aging.

Read: the procedure of maturing

Here is more about a number of those physiological changes most individuals can expect if they turn 50:

Changes in your hair and skin.

Your skin will begin to become thinner and shed excess weight and produce less oil, that can make it eventually become drier and less flexible. Few men and women escape the lumps of old and middle age, but decent skincare, and preventing sunlight, can arrest this procedure.

Hair-pigment cells will become thinner and your hair will begin to turn gray. Hair will get thinner over the entire scalp (more so in men compared to women).

Changes in sight and hearing.

Declining sight and hearing frequently comes with aging. Many middle-aged men and women need reading glasses, since it becomes increasingly more challenging for your eyes to focus on items which are shut up. One frequently sees elderly folks holding a text or thing at arm's length so as to view it even better. Some elderly folks get nervous or may grow greater stress in the fluid in the eye (glaucoma). Night vision and visual sharpness tend to decrease.

Hearing issues are frequent in elderly individuals. It frequently happens slowly, so is not always detected. With age, high sound audio become more difficult to listen to and in addition, it becomes hard to follow a conversation when there's a great deal of background sound.

Changes in sleep patterns.
1 piece of good news: elderly people need less sleep than younger people do. As you get older, you will also often wake up frequently and you won't sleep as much as you had been when you're younger.

Changes in your weight.
As you age, your body will require extra energy. If you continue eating the exact same quantity you did when you're younger, then you may lose weight. Routine exercise can help prevent weight gain. Muscle mass is diminished by age and this also slows down your metabolism also, which then can force you to pick up a couple of kilos.

Read: can your job help conserve your aging mind? Changes in heart function.

Your heartbeat slows down age, and also your arteries can become stiffer. Both of these things can place strain in the heart, and your own heart rate may become enlarged. Many elderly people develop heart problems due to these variables.

Changes in your joints and bones.

Much like all mechanical items, long-term usage triggers wear and tear. Elderly folks can develop osteoporosis, which induces bone density to be decreased. This could cause bone fractures. Many elderly people also shed a little bit of height. Osteoarthritis (whenever the cartilage at a joint wears off) can be common in people over 65. Being obese increases your risk.

Changes in bladder control.

As muscle function declines, so does bladder management. Urinary incontinence (from minor "flows" to acute bladder-control issues) influence many elderly folks, particularly girls. This is sometimes socially inhibiting. There are exercises and treatments to cure this, so all isn't lost.

The way your nutritional needs change as you get older

That is because aging is connected to many different changes, such as nutrient deficiencies, diminished quality of life and poor health effects.

Fortunately, there are things you can do in order to help prevent deficiencies along with additional curricular alterations. By way of instance, eating foods that are wholesome and choosing the right supplements might help you to stay healthy as you get older.

How can aging affect your nutritional needs?
Aging is connected to many different changes within the body, such as weight reduction, thinner skin and less stomach acidity.

A number of them changes can cause you to be more prone to nutrient deficiencies, though some can influence your perceptions and high quality of life.

By way of example, studies have estimated that 20 percent of older individuals have atrophic gastritis, a disorder where chronic inflammation gets ruined the cells which make stomach acid.

Low stomach acid may influence the absorption of nutrition, like vitamin b12, calcium, magnesium and iron.

Another challenge of aging is a decreased need for carbs. Sadly, this produces a nutritional issue. Older adults will need to have equally as much, or more, of a few nourishment, while consuming fewer calories.

Luckily, eating a number of whole foods and choosing a supplement can help you meet your nutritional supplement requirements.

Another matter folks may encounter as they age is a decrease in their own body's capacity to comprehend vital sensations like thirst and hunger.

This may create you likely to overeating and unintentional weight loss. Along with the older you get, the more harsher these impacts might be.

Aging is connected to fat loss, thinner skin along with decreased stomach acid. Your ability to understand hunger and desire might also be diminished as you get older.

 # 2 fewer calories, however nutrients
A individual's daily calorie needs depend upon their own height, weight, muscle mass, activity level and lots of different facets.

Older adults can want fewer calories to keep their weight, because they are inclined to exercise and move less and take less muscle.

Should you continue to consume exactly the identical amount of calories each day because you did when you're younger, then you might easily gain additional fat, particularly around the stomach region.

This is particularly accurate in postmenopausal women, since the decrease in estrogen levels found in this period can encourage belly fat.

But even though elderly adults want fewer calories they want equally as high or higher amounts of several nutrients, in contrast to younger individuals.

This makes it very important for elderly people to eat many different whole foods, like fruits, fish, vegetables and lean meats. These wholesome principles are able to allow you to combat nutrient deficiencies, even without increasing your waistline.

Nutrients that become particularly critical as you age comprise vitamin d, vitamin d, magnesium and vitamin b12.

Older adults generally require fewer calories. But, their nutrient demands are equally as high or higher than if they're younger. That is why ingesting salty foods that are whole becomes exceptionally important.

No one can gain from protein
It is common to lose strength and muscle as you get older.

In reality, the average adult loses 3-8 percent of the muscle mass every decade after age 30. This reduction of muscle mass and intensity is popularly referred to as sarcopenia.

It is a significant cause of fatigue, fractures and bad health among the older. Eating more protein can help your body keep muscle and combat sarcopenia.
Additionally, a summary of 20 recent research in older people discovered that consuming more protein or using protein supplements can slow down the rate of muscle development, improve muscle density and help build muscle muscle.

Furthermore, combining a protein-rich diet together with resistance training appears to be the best approach to resist sarcopenia.

You can discover lots of easy approaches to raise your protein consumption.

Eating a protein-rich diet might help combat sarcopenia, the weight reduction loss of strength and muscle. Research suggests that you will find the maximum benefits if you mix a protein-rich diet together with resistance training.

you might gain from fiber

Constipation is a common health issue among the older.

It is especially common in people over 65, and it is just two to three times more prevalent in girls.

That is because individuals in this age have a tendency to proceed and be more inclined to take drugs who have constipation as a side impact.

Eating fiber can help alleviate constipation. It moves through the intestine undigested, helping sort fences and promote regular bowel motions.

In an investigation of five research, scientists discovered that dietary fiber aids provoke bowel movements in people with gout.

In addition, a high-fiber diet can stop diverticular disease, a disease in which small pouches form over the colon and eventually become inflamed or infected. This problem is particularly common among the elderly.

Diverticular disorder is often regarded as a disorder of the diet. It is extremely common, affecting around 50 percent of individuals over age 50 in western nations.

You can find that a couple of approaches to improve your fiber consumption.

Bowel-related problems, such as constipation and cardiovascular disease, can happen as you get older. You can help protect yourself by simply increasing your fiber consumption.

you want more magnesium and vitamin d

Calcium and vitamin d are just two of the most crucial nutrients for bone health.

Magnesium aids construct and maintain healthy bones while vitamin d helps the body absorb calcium.

Regrettably, older adults have a tendency to consume less calcium in their diets.

Human and animal studies have discovered that the gut will consume less calcium in age.

However, the reduction in calcium consumption is probably caused by a vitamin deficiency, because aging may make the body not as effective at generating it.

Your system can create vitamin d in the cholesterol on your skin when it's exposed to sun.

But, aging may produce the skin fuller, and that reduces its capacity to generate vitamin d.

Collectively, these changes could keep you from getting adequate calcium and vitamin d, boosting bone loss and increasing your chance of fractures.

To counter aging's effects in your own vitamin d and calcium levels, it is required to eat more calcium and vitamin d through supplements and foods.

A number of foods contain calcium, such as dairy products and dark green and leafy veggies. It is possible to discover other excellent sources of calcium.

Meanwhile, vitamin d can be found in many different fish, including herring and salmon. It is possible to discover other fantastic resources of vitamin d.

Older folks can also gain from using a vitamin d supplement such as cod liver oil.

Calcium and vitamin d are vital nutrients for maintaining optimum bone health. Your entire body stands to profit from becoming more calcium along with vitamin d as you get older.

you might want more vitamin b12

Vitamin b12 is a water-soluble vitamin also called cobalamin.

It is crucial for producing red blood cells and maintaining healthy brain functioning.

Regrettably, studies indicate that 10--30 percent of individuals over age 50 have a diminished capacity to absorb vitamin b12 in their daily diet.

Over the years, this could give rise to a vitamin b12 deficiency.

Vitamin b12 in the diet plan is bound to proteins from the food that you consume. Before your body can utilize it, gut acid has to allow it to different from these types of meals proteins.
Older people are more likely to get illnesses that decrease stomach acid production, resulting in less vitamin b12 absorption in meals. Atrophic gastritis is 1 condition that could lead to this.

Additionally, older individuals who follow a vegetarian or vegan diet are not as inclined to consume abundant sources of vitamin b12, as it is more plentiful in animal foods such as fish, eggs, dairy and meat.

Because of this, older folks may gain from using a vitamin b12 supplement or ingesting foods fortified with vitamin b12.

These fortified foods include crystalline vitamin b12, which isn't bound to fats. So individuals who make less than the standard quantity of stomach acid may still consume it.

Aging increases the danger of a vitamin b12 deficiency. Older adults may particularly benefit from using a vitamin b12 supplement or consuming foods fortified with vitamin b12.

you're more prone into dehydration

Water constitutes roughly 60 percent of the physique.
It is important to remain hydrated at any given point, ever since your body regularly sheds water, chiefly through perspiration and urine.

Additionally, aging can make you more prone to dehydration.

Your body finds appetite through receptors within the brain and throughout the body.
But as you era, these receptors might be less vulnerable to water fluctuations, making it more challenging for them to discover thirst.

Additionally, your kidneys assist your body preserve water, however they are inclined to eliminate function as you get older.
Regrettably, dehydration includes unpleasant consequences for elderly people.

Long-term dehydration can lessen the fluid from your tissues, lowering your capacity to consume medication, worsening medical illnesses along with raising exhaustion (4).
That is why it's important to generate a conscious attempt to consume sufficient water every day. Should you find drinking water a struggle, try using one to 2 glasses of water with every meal.

Otherwise, consider carrying out a water jar as you go about daily.

Drinking an adequate quantity of water is equally essential as you get older, as the body will be able to understand the signals of dehydration.

You might glad to eat enough food

Another troubling concern for older people is diminished appetite.

If this matter isn't addressed, it may result in accidental weight loss and nutritional deficiencies. A loss of appetite can also be linked to bad health and a greater chance of death.

Factors which may cause older adults to have a bad appetite comprise changes in hormones, flavour and odor, in addition to changes in life conditions.

Studies have discovered that elderly people have a tendency to have reduced levels of desire hormones and high degrees of fullness hormones, so they could acquire hungry less frequently and feel fuller longer quickly.

In a small research with 11 older individuals and 11 young adults, researchers found that older participants had significantly reduced rates of the hunger hormone ghrelin prior to a meal.

Additionally, many studies have found that older individuals have higher degrees of their fullness hormones cholecystokinin and leptin.

Aging may also change your sense of taste and odor, which makes foods look less attractive.

Other facets which might cause poor appetite comprise tooth loss, solitude, inherent illness and drugs that could reduce appetite.

If you discover it hard to consume huge meals, consider dividing your foods into smaller parts and also consume them every couple of hours.

Otherwise, attempt to set a custom of eating healthful snacks such as almonds, boiled and yogurt eggs, that provide a lot of nourishment and many of calories.

How to keep your bones strong as you age

It's true that individuals shed bone as we age. Bone loss can lead to osteoporosis, where bones may get so thin they split. Fractures from osteoporosis are a chief cause of disability. The good news: osteoporosis is not a normal part of aging there's plenty you can do to keep your muscles healthy and strong.

The first step is getting all of the nutrients you require for good bone growth. "a nutritious diet can significantly lower the risk of bone loss and obesity, "and it's never too late to get started."

Bone power goes beyond the nutrition basics

Healthy bones depend on over calcium and we now know that many nutrients are crucial to maintaining bone. "unfortunately, the diets of most elderly people fall short on a number of those nutrients. "so even though they are becoming calcium and vitamin d, they're still losing bone"

A diet of whole foods

The best way to get all the nutrients you need is to fill out your plate with whole foods. Nuts, legumes, whole grains, legumes and vegetables and fruit are naturally abundant in a range of nutrients vital to healthy bones. Fruits and vegetables are equally as essential as dairy product for bone health.

Selecting nutrient-rich foods is especially important as you get older because most people's calorie requirements move down. "the challenge is to become as much nourishment into a limited number of calories.

Avoid highly processed foods. Processing strips several foods of their natural nutrients. Even when vitamins or minerals are added back, processed foods generally lack the full collection of nutrients found in natural foods.

Choose whole foods. Whenever you have the option, go for meals with whole grains, which are much richer in nutrients linked to bone health. Consider the ingredient panel of breads, cereals, and other products produced with grain. The first component should be a whole grain.

Go for variety." particularly if you're cooking for yourself, then it's easy to get stuck in a rut. That rut can indicate you're missing out on the variety that ensures a nutritious diet." try a new grain, like bulgur or quinoa. Choose vegetables from across the spectrum of colors, from leafy greens into red sweet peppers. A diet that is vibrant, nutritionists say, will help to ensure a balance of nutrients required for good bone health.

When to attain for calcium or vitamin d supplements

Even the healthiest diet may not provide all the nutrients you need for bone health. If you do not consume milk, for instance, you could be falling short on calcium. Multivitamins or only supplements of certain nutrients can help fill the gaps. But before you begin taking any nutritional supplement, it's wise to speak with your physician.

Five crucial strategies for bone maintenance following 50

Osteoporosis is a disease in which bones become fragile and weak, leading to an increased risk of fractures (broken bones). People with osteoporosis may undergo a fracture after a slight bulge, or even a fall from standing height, in the course of daily actions. Osteoporosis has no signs or symptoms until a fracture occurs -- this is why it's often called a 'silent disease'. Fractures due to osteoporosis occur most commonly at sites like the wrist, upper arm, pelvis, spine and hip, and can lead to acute pain, significant disability and even death.

Bone health matters

In most nations and civilizations, women play a very important part in the household and in society. Women over age 50 specifically face a growing burden of responsibilities; as caregivers to the old and young, bread champions preparing for retirement and contributors to the welfare of those communities in which they reside. Fragility fractures exact a horrible toll on the quality of life of postmenopausal women worldwide. Everyone knows a family member or friend that has suffered an osteoporotic fracture; whether a 55-year-old sister who has broken her wrist or a 78- year-old grandmother who's broken her hip. Each these women's lives will be severely affected by fractures. Because osteoporosis is so common, every woman must come to recognize that bone health really matters to her and the welfare of her family.

Postmenopausal girls

Postmenopausal girls are at high risk of developing osteoporosis and suffering fractures on account of the rapid bone loss which occurs with the start of menopause. Bone mass peaks at the mid-twenties and remains relatively stable until the beginning of menopause, which occurs between age 50 and 53 in women from Europe and north America, as early as age 42 in Latin America and Asia.

Oestrogen plays with a vital part in regulating bone production and turnover during life. Each day our skeletons undergo a procedure for breakdown and formation. However, as women become oestrogen paralyzed when menses stop, bone dysfunction starts to exceed bone formation. Besides oestrogen deficiency, reduced intestinal calcium intake, increases urinary calcium reduction, and loss of bone protective hormones also have a negative impact on bone health. Menopause-induced bone loss is most acute in women who've had their ovaries surgically removed or at cancer patients who have experienced aromatase inhibitor treatment

Five essential strategies

Your threat of growing osteoporosis and fragility fractures is set by a number of factors, a few of which may be transformed (e.g. Exercise, nutrition and smoking) while others cannot (e.g.
Family history, age at menopause and ailments like rheumatoid arthritis).while peak bone mass can be highly genetically determined, after 65 years of age genetics play a diminishing role in bone loss and other things, such as nutrition and exercise, play an increasingly significant function.

Maintaining a healthy skeleton involves five crucial strategies to lessen your risk of osteoporosis and fractures.

Strategy 1; exercise regularly

The expression 'move it or lose it' is not more true than after age 50. At menopause, exercise becomes especially critical for the maintenance of bone mass and muscle power. Besides maintaining bone strength, the main goal of exercise is to increase muscle mass in order to boost muscle function, and to maintain decent balance and endurance. Weak muscles and poor balance may lead to falls and fractures.

The positive impact of exercise on bone is dependent upon both the type of exercise and the intensity. Resistance (or muscle-strengthening) exercises become much more important as one ages. Although it isn't simple to construct bone mineral after adulthood, exercise has been shown to lead to modest increases in bone mineral density (bmd) of around 1-2%.exercise programmes should be tailored to your own wants and capacities, particularly in the event that you have osteoporosis, have been highly prone to falling, or are brittle.

Exercises for healthy postmenopausal women who do not have osteoporosis

In general, you should aim to exercise for 30 to 40 minutes, three to four times per week, with some weight-bearing and resistance exercises at the programme. Some examples include;

Weight bearing

- dancing
- high-impact aerobics
- trekking
- jogging/running
- jumping rope
- stair climbing §tennis Muscle strengthen
- lifting weights
- employing flexible exercise bands
- using weight machines
- lifting your own body fat

- standing and climbing on your toes

Balance, posture and practical exercises also have a significant function to play

Balance exercises that strengthen the thighs and also examine your equilibrium can reduce falls danger, e.g. Tai chi

Posture exercises to improve posture and reduce curved shoulders can decrease fracture risk, especially at the backbone

Functional exercises; exercises that help with everyday tasks

Exercise for women with osteoporosis

If you've osteoporosis, your workout plan should specifically target balance, posture, gait, coordination, and fashionable and back stabilization rather than general aerobic fitness. An individually targeted exercise programme, with oversight if required, assists recovery of function, helps prevent additional afield drops, and improves quality of life.

The next should be prevented if you have osteoporosis
- sit-ups and excessive bending in the waist (can cause vertebral crush fractures)
- twisting movements (such as a golf swing)
- exercises that involve sudden or volatile loading, or high-intensity loading (like jumps)
- daily activities like bending to pick up things (can cause vertebral crush fractures)

Strategy 2; ensure a healthy diet

A balanced diet that includes sufficient calcium, vitamin d, protein, and other bone-healthy nourishment is an essential ingredient for good bone health. Below is a listing of the key nutrients that lead to strong and healthy muscles and bones.

Calcium

Magnesium is a major building block of our skeleton. The calcium in our bones additionally acts as a reservoir to maintaining calcium levels in the bloodstream, which is crucial for nerve and muscle function. As the body's ability to absorb calcium declines with advancing age, a female's needs will increase. Recommended calcium intake varies country to country, however most of health authorities recognize the increased need for calcium in postmenopausal women and elderly adults

Strategy 3; avoid negative lifestyle

The negative habits that affect your overall health and have a negative influence on your bone health, and also raise your risk of fractures and osteoporosis.

Smoking

Latest smokers and people who have smoked within the past are at higher risk of any fracture, compared to non-smokers. Excessive alcohol intake.

Alcohol taken in moderation -- e.g. Around two glasses (2 x 120 ml) of wine per day -- does not adversely impact bone health. But, long-term heavy alcohol use was shown to increase fracture risk in both men and women in that it affects bone forming tissues and hormones, raises risk of falls, and is related to poor nutrition connected to magnesium, vitamin d or protein.

Maintaining a healthful weight

Getting underweight is associated with greater bone loss and increased risk of fracture. People with a bmi of 20 kg/m2 have a two-fold increased risk of fracture compared to individuals having a bmi of 25 kg/m2. Make sure your foods offer enough caloric intake and the nutrition you need to keep healthy muscles and bones.

Strategy 4; describe your risk factors

To enable you and your physician to identify if you may be at elevated risk of enduring osteoporotic fractures, you should be aware of the subsequent 'nonmodifiable' threat factors:

Past fragility fractures

Anyone over age 50 who has experienced a previous fracture is at double the probability of a future fracture in contrast to someone who hasn't fractured. In actuality, half of patients who suffer hip fractures have broken another bone prior to breaking up their hip. If you have already suffered a fragility fracture, then it's critically important that you talk about how to prevent future fractures with your physician.

Family history of osteoporosis and fractures
Genetics will ascertain your peak possible bone density and the rate of bone loss from the early years after menopause. A parental history of fracture is associated with a heightened risk of fracture that is independent of bone mineral density. If your parents have endured hip fractures happen to be diagnosed with osteoporosis you are at greater risk.

Menopause

What's menopause?

Menopause is your end of a woman's menstrual cycles. The term could clarify any of these changes you undergo before or after you stop getting your period, marking the conclusion of your reproductive years.

Menopause causes

A girl is born with all of her eggs that are stored in her ovaries. The ovaries also produce the hormones estrogen and progesterone, which regulate period (menstruation) along with the release of eggs (ovulation). Menopause happens when the ovaries no longer release an egg each month and ovulation stops.

Menopause is a normal part of aging when it happens after the age of 40. However, some women can undergo menopause early. It can be the consequence of surgery, like if their ovaries are removed in a hysterectomy, or harm to their own clitoris, such as in chemotherapy. If it happens before age 40, for that reason, it is known as premature menopause.

What conditions cause premature menopause?

Your genes, some immune system disorders, or medical procedures can cause premature menopause. Other reasons include:

- premature ovarian failure. When your ovaries prematurely stop releasing eggs, for unknown reasons, your levels of estrogen and progesterone change. While this occurs before you're 40, it is known as premature ovarian failure. Unlike premature menopause, premature ovarian failure isn't always permanent.

- induced menopause. This happens whenever your doctor takes out your ovaries for medical reasons, such as esophageal cancer or even endometriosis. In addition, it can occur when radiation or even chemotherapy damages your ovaries.

Menopause process

Natural menopause is not caused by any type of medical or surgical treatment. It's slow and contains three stages:

- perimenopause. This phase usually begins several years before menopause, when your embryo gradually generate less estrogen. Perimenopause continues until menopause, the stage where your ovaries stop releasing eggs. In the last 1 to 2 years of the period, estrogen levels drop faster. Many women have menopause symptoms.

- menopause. That is when it has been a year since you had a period. Your ovaries have ceased releasing eggs and producing the majority of the estrogen.

- postmenopause. All these are the years following menopause. Menopausal symptoms like sexy flashes generally facilitate. But health risks related to the loss of estrogen increase as you become older.

Menopause symptoms

Most girls nearing menopause will possess hot flashes, surprising feelings of warmth that spread over the upper body, frequently with blushing and sweating. These flashes can vary from mild in most girls to severe others.

Additional symptoms contain:

- Uneven or missed periods

- Insomnia

- Mood swings

- Fatigue

- Depression

- Crankiness

- Swaying core

- Trainers

- Joint and muscular aches and pains

- Changes in libido (sex push)

- Vaginal dryness

- Trouble controlling your bladder

- Menopause diagnosis

You may guess that you're going into melancholy. Or your health care provider will state something, according to symptoms you've told them around.

Continue reading below

You can keep track of your sessions and graph them as they become uneven. The pattern will be another hint to your physician that you are menopausal.

Your doctor might also test your blood to degrees of:

Follicle-stimulating hormone (fsh). This usually goes up as you near menopause. Estradiol. This tells your doctor how far estrogen your ovaries are making.

Immune hormones. This reveals problems with your thyroid gland, which may impact your period and lead to symptoms that seem like menopause.

Menopause remedy

Menopause is a natural procedure. Many symptoms will go away as time passes. However, if they're causing problems, treatments can allow you to feel better. Frequent ones include:

Hormone replacement therapy (hrt). This can also be called menopausal hormone therapy. You take medications to replace the hormones your body isn't making anymore. Particular drugs or combinations can help with hot flashes and vaginal disease, as well as creating your muscles stronger. But they are also able to put you at greater risk of medical problems such as cardiovascular disease or breast feeding, which means you need to take the smallest dose which works for the shortest time possible.

Topical hormone therapy. This really is an herbal cream, add, or gel that you place in your vagina to help with dryness.

Nonhormone medications. The melancholy drug paroxetine (brisdelle, paxil) is fda-approved to deal with hot flashes. The nerve drug gabapentin (gralise, neuraptine, neurontin) and the blood pressure medication clonidine (catapres, kapvay) may also facilitate them. Medicines called selective estrogen receptor modulators (serms) help your body use its estrogen to treat hot flashes and vaginal dryness.

Medicines for osteoporosis. You may take drugs or vitamin d supplements to help keep your bones strong.

Lifestyle changes help many women cope with menopause symptoms. Try these steps:

If you're having hot flashes, then drink cold water, then sit or sleep near a fan, and then dress in layers.

Utilize an over-the-counter vaginal lubricant or moisturizer for dryness.

Exercise often to sleep and prevent ailments like cardiovascular disease, diabetes, and osteoporosis.

Strengthen your pelvic floor muscles with kegel exercises to avoid bladder leaks. Stay socially and mentally active to avoid memory problems.

Don't smoke. Tobacco might cause early menopause and increase hot flashes.

Limit how much alcohol you consume, to lower your probability of getting breast cancer also allow you to sleep better.

Eat a variety of foods and maintain a healthy weight to assist with hot flashes. Practice things like yoga, deep breathing, or massage that will help you unwind.

Some studies have found that soy products relieve hot flashes, however, researchers are still looking into it. There is little to no evidence that other supplements work for menopause symptoms. Talk with your health care provider before starting any herbal or dietary supplements.

Menopause complications

The reduction of estrogen associated with menopause is tied to a number of health issues that become more common as women age.

Following menopause, women are more likely to possess:

- Bone reduction (osteoporosis)
- Heart disorder
- Bladder and bowels which don't function like they ought to
- Higher chance of alzheimer's disease
- More wrinkles

- Poor muscle power and tone
- Weaker vision, such as from cataracts (clouding of the lens of this eye) and macular degeneration (breakdown of this small area in the middle of the retina that's the middle of vision)
- What causes muscle wasting?
- Muscle atrophy

Muscle atrophy is when muscles waste away. It's usually brought on by too little physical activity.

When a disorder or harm makes it hard or impossible for you to move an arm or leg, so the lack of freedom could lead to muscle wasting. Over time, without routine movement, your arm or leg can start to seem smaller but much shorter than the one you're ready to move.

In some cases, muscle wasting could be reversed using a suitable diet, exercise, or physical treatment.

Symptoms of muscle atrophy

You will have muscle atrophy if:

One of your arms or legs is markedly smaller than the other.

You are experiencing noticeable weakness in one limb. You've been inactive for a very long time.

Call your physician to schedule a complete medical exam if you think you might have muscle atrophy or whether you're unable to proceed normally. You might have an undiagnosed condition that needs treatment.

Reasons of muscle atrophy

Unused muscles can squander away if you are not active. But even after it begins, this kind of atrophy may often be reversed with exercise and improved nutrition.

Muscle atrophy can also take place if you are bedridden or not able to move certain body parts due to a medical condition. Astronauts, by way of example, can experience muscle atrophy after a couple of days of weightlessness.

Other causes for muscle atrophy include:

- Deficiency of physical action for a protracted period of time

- Aging

- Alcohol-associated myopathy, a pain and weakness in muscles due to excess drinking over long periods of time

- Burns

- Injuries, including a torn rotator cuff or broken bones

- Malnutrition

- Spinal cord or peripheral nerve injuries

- Stroke

- Long-term corticosteroid treatment

Some medical conditions can cause muscles to waste away or can cause movement difficult, resulting in muscle atrophy. These include:

- Amyotrophic lateral sclerosis (als), also called lou gehrig's disease, affects nerve cells which control voluntary muscle movement
- Dermatomyositis, causes muscle weakness and skin rash
- Guillain-barré illness, an autoimmune disease that contributes to nerve inflammation and muscular fatigue
- Multiple sclerosis, an autoimmune disease where the body destroys the protective coverings of nerves
- Muscular dystrophy, an inherited condition that causes muscle fatigue
- Neuropathy, damage to a nerve or nerve group, leading to loss of sensation or function
- Osteoarthritis, causes reduced motion in the joints
- Polio, a viral illness affecting muscle tissue which may lead to paralysis
- Polymyositis, an inflammatory illness
- Rheumatoid arthritis, a chronic inflammatory autoimmune disease that affects the joints
- Spinal muscle atrophy, an hereditary condition causing arm and leg muscles to waste

How is muscle atrophy diagnosed?

If muscle atrophy is caused by another state, you might want to undergo testing to diagnose the problem.

Your doctor will ask your whole medical history. You will likely be requested to:

Tell them about old or old injuries and previously diagnosed medical conditions List prescriptions, over-the counter drugs, and supplements you're taking Provide a comprehensive outline of your symptoms

Your doctor may additionally order tests to help with the analysis and to rule out specific ailments. These tests can include:

- Blood evaluations

- X-rays

- Magnetic resonance imaging (mri)

- Computed tomography (ct) scanning

- Nerve conduction research

- Muscle or nerve biopsy

- Electromyography (emg)

Your doctor may consult with a specialist depending on the results of those evaluations.

How is muscle atrophy handled?

Treatment will rely on your diagnosis and the severity of your muscle building. Any underlying medical conditions have to be addressed. Frequent treatments for muscle atrophy contain:

- Exercise

- Physical therapy

- Ultrasound treatment

- Surgery

- Dietary modifications

Physical therapists can teach you the appropriate strategies to exercise. They can also transfer your arms and legs for you in case you have problems moving.

Ultrasound treatment is a non-invasive procedure that uses sound waves to assist in healing.

If your joints, ligaments, skin, or muscles are too tight and prevent you from transferring, surgery might be necessary. This problem is known as contracture deformity.

Surgery could be able to correct contracture deformity if your muscular atrophy is a result of malnutrition. It may likewise have the ability to correct your condition if a ripped tendon triggered your muscle atrophy.

If malnutrition is the reason behind muscle atrophy, your physician may suggest dietary changes or supplements.

Weight gain tips: 19 approaches to gain weight fast One main concern to our thin friends is that gaining weight the ideal way may be a daunting task for them. This is simply because, when they really do lose weight, it should be evenly spread in their entire body instead of only concentrated in the abdominal area.

There are lots of reasons because of which one may be underweight: inadequate eating habits, protracted meal period interruptions, inadequate selection of foods, regardless of suitable amount of calorie intake in and calorie out, malabsorption of foods that they are presently eating, prolonged diseases and suffering from eating disorders like anorexia nervosa or bulimia.

It's vital to understand that gaining weight the ideal way and not by tapping on unhealthy foods is a better choice for your body to save yourself from being prone to ailments like diabetes and thyroid, which even the happiest individual in a room may get. This is due to indulging in unhealthy foods, you are also developing a nutrition deficiency, which may cause lifestyle problems like thyroid and diabetes.

Following are tips and tips one must bear in mind whilst trying to gain weight in a healthful manner.

1.   Individuals may be underweight due to various reasons: like mentioned previously, understanding your own body prior to starting anything is essential. The very first thing is to get to the origin of the problem. Knowing why your system isn't able to obtain weight is necessary. Consult your nutritionist along with your physician to analyse the core issue.

2.   Healthful weight gain: as indians, if we are thin, we are frequently told to eat anything and everything, as 'nothing gets used in our own body'. However, this perception needs to stop. A gradual weight reduction is permanent and wholesome one. Increasing your everyday intake by 500kcal per day can cause your body gaining 0.5 kgs every week. But this entirely depends upon how your body responds to different foods, you gender, present body weight and height.

3.   Exercise: the biggest mistake a thin person can make is to presume that no meals will impact their body. The thinnest bodies tend to find a unsightly paunch and it's important not to get to the point. This is since a paunch simply means that the circulatory and the subcutaneous fat on the human body are increasing, which is not a healthy sign. In addition to this, it is also a sign that you may slowly be leading towards weaker muscles. Because of this, it's important to participate in a mixture of cardio, weight training and flexibility improving exercises every day.

4.   Lift weights for lean mass: in other words, this means the amount of weight your body communicates, which is not fat. Hence, the ultimate purpose is to increase lean body weight. For this, you'll have to indulge in some significant weight lifting. This ought to include exercises like squats, deadlifts, presses, pull-ups, rows, drops, snatches, cleans and jerks. These exercises can help in engaging multiple muscles while still activating your hormonal response systems.

5.   Exercises for newcomers:

A

- Squat 5x5
- Pull-ups 5x5
- Overhead press 5x5

B

- Squat 5x5
- Deadlift 1/2/3x5 (your selection; deadlifts can be incredibly reckless, as well as fatigue comes poor kind, so be cautious; sometimes it is better to do some really heavy load for one group)

- Bench press 5x5

C

- Squat 5x5
- Pull up 5x5
- Overhead press 5x5

Do this arrangement weekly (possibly monday, wednesday, friday) and steadily increase the weight each session. Once you're making progress, feel free to add in other exercises such as drops or more olympic lifts.

6.   Healthful diet: the sector is packed with dietary supplements, which may promise you weight gain very quickly. However, it's very important to bear in mind that many of these nutritional supplements are full of artificial nutrition, which may acquire weight temporarily but destroy your health forever. Therefore, ask your nutritionist or family physician before consuming something. Secondly, these supplements will merely come in handy when your diet plan is in place. Your body demands the right amount of proteins, fats and carbs. Sticking to a healthy diet saturated in both nuts and dairy products and exclusive of alcohol will allow you to get faster results.

7.   Nutritious heart and weight reduction dieta significant mistake the majority of us wind up making, in our effort to obtain weight is eating foods which can harm us. We want healthy fat in our own body and consuming empty calories total of unhealthy fats will only deplete our wellness. So, include healthy snacks on your diet. This implies nuts, fruits, fruits, dry snacks such as roasted chana will probably be exceedingly valuable in gaining weight within a healthy manner. Apart from this, you may also indulge in multigrain breads, soy sticks,

hummus and peanut butter (all of which are full of protein). Choosing fiber rich foods will also be good for you. The absolute most crucial point to remember is that the size of your desire should increase gradually.

8.   Eat less: another large myth for thin people that needs to be busted right manner is consuming foods in huge amounts to gain weight. Consuming crap foods in huge quantities and supposing your body will be unaffected by it's foolish. The perfect method to go about gaining weight would be to divide your foods into smaller pieces, to prevent snacking. It's a better choice to go for foods which are calorie and nutrient dense compared to foods which are loaded with unhealthy calories. A lean person who indulges in unhealthy eating habits would be as vulnerable to lifestyle ailments as any obese person.

9.   Indulge the right way: as mentioned previously, indulgence ought to be done the proper way. When getting on any fitness travel, whether to lose or gain weight, then our ears are filled with many different opinions. One such opinion for lean folks would be to eat as many sweet foods because possible. Not only can this increase the visceral fat (fat throughout your organs), but will also cause malabsorption of nutrients from other foods in our own body. The largest concern for a lanky person is to become fat in the incorrect places.

10.   Include vegetables and meats: vegetables and meats are abundant sources of antioxidants, fiber and minerals. All these are important for a person seeking to gain weight. Including vegetables and meats will also help you to stay away from unhealthy snacks because these help to curb hunger pangs. We need to supply our body with sufficient protein for the hormones to synthesize.

11.   Eat healthier fats: the ideal way to add healthy fats in your daily diet is by eating egg yolks, meats with animal fats, coconut oil, and other healthful fats. Including fruits like bananas and sapodilla can help as well. On the other hand, the consumption of them should be in moderation.

12.   Boost protein ingestion: the ideal intake for virtually any body, regardless of being lean or obese or wholesome, is just 1 gm/kg. Here is the fundamental requirement which should be fulfilled on a daily basis. Not only can this suppress your unnecessary hinger pangs that make you hog on unhealthy foods, but in addition, it helps you keep a healthy body weight with lean body mass. Proteins are the building blocks of the body and when your system starves of it, then it will never be able to realize its most healthy best. Including tofu, paneer, chicken, and vegetables like spinach will enable you to get through with your everyday protein consumption.

13.   Eat foods that assist you to gain weight: there are natural foods that make you lose weight in a wholesome way. Adding foods full of healthy fat content is vital. You are able to incorporate fish such as tuna and salmon, organic fruit juices, whole wheat noodles and indian breads.

14.   Foods rich in calories: there are two unique types of carbs: empty and wholesome. Empty calories are those that we get away from processed foods and liquids, while healthy calories would be those that we get from organic foods such as vegetables and fruits. Some examples are cheeses, oils, peanuts, home made butters such as vanilla and peanut butters.

15.   Daily tips: to be able to add weight, it's suggested to stick to some basics. For example, do not load your plate with unnecessary foods like chocolate bars and canned

juices, merely to get weight quickly. Including healthy foods like yoghurt will help you gaining weight gradually but permanently. Including three to four servings of produce on a daily basis won't just help you suppress your appetite for unhealthy foods but may also provide you with required nutrients.

16.   Dietary nutritional supplements for gaining weight: dietary supplements comprises pills, capsules and powders. These are able to be protein powders, meal replacement bars, multivitamins etc.. As stated earlier, ingestion of some of them ought to be carried out only after consulting your physician or nutritionist. Excess of dietary supplements may cause different problems like nausea and diarrhoea. Though they are wanted in the modern times, it's almost always preferable to find consultation on particular goods.

17.   Food habits: eating one wholesome meal and 3 bad ones will just slower the procedure for you and can result in health risks. Some principles to recall are: cooking your food correctly to boost digestion, preventing excessive consumption of carbonated beverages and alcohol since it disrupts the absorption of nourishment, keeping tabs on your own weight and cooking your own meals with options which are beneficial for your health.

18.   Unhealthy customs for gaining healthful weight: as mentioned previously, lean or thin men and women have a tendency to have misconceptions about being 'healthy'. Being healthy doesn't imply being fat for lean people and vice-versa. Some bad habits you'll need to erase away are:

-skipping breakfast

-eating foods at odd times

-going on wreck foods

- eating a lot of crap

- finishing food due to peer pressure

- insufficient sleep

19.   The ending result: in the close of the day, your final goal must be to obtain weight wherein your own body is curved and toned in the ideal places. As a lean person, if you're gaining weight around your abdominal region, then there's an problem.

Why you have to adhere to a diet following 50

3 diet affects women over 50 must make at the moment

1. Calcium for bone health

Osteoporosis has got a reasonable amount of focus, and many elderly girls see that the danger of creating this bone disorder increases with age. In reality, 1 in 3 women over 50 is at risk of a bone fracture brought on by osteoporosis. Osteoporosis affects men, also, but not in these high prices.

"we consume less calcium as we get older, and a few women's capacity to tolerate milk - - the top sources of calcium also decreases as they become older. "dark leafy greens and calcium-fortified orange juice along with other excellent sources."

Women over 50 need 1,200 mg of calcium every day. Use the nutrition facts label on food items to keep an eye on your consumption.

2. Protein for healthful muscle mass

Older women tend to sit, exercise less. That compounds a natural aging process named sarcopenia, that's the reduction of muscle mass. From the time girls near 80 decades, they might have dropped up to half of the skeletal muscle mass. Eating enough protein lessens the effects of the muscle wasting.

"healthy plant-based diets which don't contain beef, a significant source of protein, may still offer lots of protein should you create informed choices. He advocates picking more soy, quinoa, eggs, nuts, legumes, seeds and legumes.

Your protein needs depend on how much you weigh. For women over 50, specialists urge 1 to

1.5 g of protein per kilogram of fat (1 kilogram = 2.2 lbs). If you weigh 140 lbs, for example, you might need at least 63 g of protein every day.

3. Vitamin b-12 for brain work

As women age, they consume fewer nutrients from their food. 1 key nutrient they might not be consuming sufficient vitamin b-12, that is vital for keeping both healthy red blood cells and brain function.

"the ideal sources of vitamin b-12 include legumes, milk, lean meats, fish and fortified foods such as grains and cereals. "vegans, in particular, will have to select more refined foods, but elderly men and women who consume all foods might have trouble consuming enough vitamin b-12."

While the recommended daily consumption of vitamin b-12 for women over 50 is 2.4 micrograms every day, you should speak to your physician to find out in the event that you also require a supplement.

Three tips to help girls over 50 receive the nourishment they require.
Make whole foods that the base of your daily diet. "focusing on whole grains, veggies and fruits will help prevent a great deal of common issues that come with age.
Drink before you are thirsty. The way that your body finds hunger affects as you get older. "be sure to drink loads of water, even in the event that you don't feel hungry. Take a water bottle, and then drink a glass with each meal."

Chapter two Ketogenic diet basics

What is a ketogenic diet?

The ketogenic diet is a really low carb, high-fat diet which shares many similarities with the atkins and low-carb diets.

It entails drastically reducing carbohydrate consumption and substituting it with fat. This decrease in carbohydrates puts your system into a metabolic condition called ketosis.

When this happens, your system gets exceptionally efficient at burning fat. Additionally, it turns fat into ketones in the liver, which may supply energy to the mind.

Ketogenic diets can cause huge reductions in blood glucose and insulin levels. This, together with the enhanced ketones, has many health benefits

Different kinds of ketogenic diets

There are several variations of the ketogenic diet plan, such as:

1. Conventional ketogenic diet (skd): this really is a really low carb, moderate-protein and high fat diet. It generally contains 75 percent fat, 20% protein and only 5 percent carbohydrates.

2. Cyclical ketogenic diet (ckd): this diet involves periods of higher-carb refeeds, for example 5 ketogenic days followed by two high-carb days.

3. Targeted ketogenic diet (tkd): this diet plan lets you add carbohydrates around workouts.

4. High-protein ketogenic diet this resembles a typical ketogenic diet, however, contains additional protein. The ratio is usually 60 percent fat, 35% protein and 5 percent carbohydrates.

5. But only the standard and low-fat ketogenic diets are studied extensively. Cyclical or concentrated ketogenic diets are somewhat more complex approaches and chiefly used by athletes or bodybuilders.

The ketogenic diet is a low carb, high-fat diet which involves radically reducing carbohydrate consumption and substituting it with fatloss. The decrease in carbohydrates puts the body in a metabolic state called ketosis. Throughout the ketosis procedure the body becomes really effective at burning fat for energy and at precisely the exact same time turns fat into ketones in the liver providing energy to the mind.

On a ketogenic diet your whole body switches its own fuel source to operate almost completely on fat. Sugar decreasing hormone levels become very low, and fat burning increases radically. The diet promotes rapid weight loss more efficiently than most other diets since it instructs your body to burn fat more effectively by inputting a metabolic condition instead of just cutting out carbs, sugar products or decreasing calories that most ordinary diets go by.

The diet can easily be adapted to match with a raw vegan diet. In the lifeco, we've got a raw plant established ketogenic application -- a nourishment program where the body receives all of its energy from plant-based fats rather than carbohydrates and sugar.

Who will do the ketogenic diet?

The ketogenic diet is acceptable for many people except those with chronic health issues particularly those on drugs are advised to seek medical care before beginning the diet. It isn't recommended for people including pregnant girls, kids, individuals at risk of hypoglycemia, individuals with an extremely low bmi, and people with ailments that a ketogenic diet can exacerbate.

Benefits

The ketogenic diet is a powerful tool for people who wish to eliminate weight due to the dramatic reduction in carbohydrate intake that forces the body to burn fat rather than carbohydrates for energy.

There is even science-based speculation a keto diet can increase wellbeing and help treat or decrease the probability of cancer.

- Mental clarity and raised cognition
- Increased energy amounts
- Less appetite

- Steady blood sugar levels from small to no ingestion of carbohydrates

- Improved skin particularly for anyone who have acne

- Enriched cholesterol and cholesterol levels

- Hormone regulation and not as severe pms symptoms

What you can not consume

- Grains -- wheat, corn, cereal, rice, etc..

- Sugar -- honey, agave, maple syrup, etc..

- Fruit -- apples, bananas etc..

- Root veg -- potato, yams, etc..

What you could eat

- Leafy greens -- spinach, kale, etc..

- Above ground vegetables including broccoli, cauliflower, etc..

- Nuts and seeds macadamias, walnuts, sunflower seeds, etc..

- Avocado and berries -- raspberries, blackberries, and other low glycemic influence berries

What is ketosis?

Ketosis is a metabolic condition where your body utilizes fat and ketones instead of sugar (glucose) as its principal fuel source.

Glucose is stored on your liver and published as necessary for energy. But after carb ingestion has been exceptionally low for one or two days, these sugar stores become depleted. Your liver can earn some sugar from amino acids from the protein that you consume by means of a process called gluconeogenesis, but not nearly sufficient to fulfil the requirements of your mind, which demands a continuous fuel source.1

Luckily, ketosis can supply you with an alternate supply of energy.

In ketosis, your body produces ketones in a rapid rate. Ketones, or ketone bodies, are created from the liver from fat that you consume and your body fat. Both ketone bodies are beta- hydroxybutyrate (bhb), acetoacetate, and acetone (though acetone is a breakdown product of acetoacetate).2

Your liver actually generates ketones on a regular basis even if ingesting a higher-carb diet. This occurs mostly overnight as you sleep but generally only in tiny quantities. But, when sugar and insulin levels fall on a carb-restricted diet, the liver ramps up its production of ketones so as to offer energy to your brain.

Although both fasting plus a keto diet plan will permit you to accomplish ketosis, just a keto diet plan is sustainable over long intervals. In reality, it seems to be a healthful way to eat people have the potential to follow forever.

Benefits of ketosis

Along with supplying a renewable energy supply, ketones -- and specifically bhb -- may decrease inflammation and oxidative stress, which are thought to play a part in the development of several chronic ailments.

Really, there are several recognized advantages and possible advantages of being in supplements ketosis.

Launched advantages:

Appetite law: among the first things people often notice when they are in ketosis is they're not hungry all of the time. Actually, studies have demonstrated that being in ketosis suppresses appetite.

1 study looked at individuals who lost weight by following a ketogenic diet for eight months and then reintroduced little quantities of carbohydrates. The researchers noted that levels of ghrelin (the "hunger hormone") were suppressed in people who stayed in ketosis, whereas individuals who were no more in ketosis had greater ghrelin levels.

Weight reduction: a lot of individuals automatically consume less when they limit carbs and are permitted as much protein and fat as they want to feel complete. Since ketogenic diets suppress hunger, reduce glucose levels, and increase fat burning, it's not surprising that they have been proven to outperform several other diets meant for weight reduction. Reversal of diabetes and prediabetes: in individuals with type 2 diabetes or prediabetes, being in ketosis will help normalize blood glucose and insulin response, possibly resulting in the discontinuation of diabetes drugs.

Potentially improved athletic performance: ketosis can offer a very long-lasting fuel source during sustained exercise in equally recreational and high-income athletes.

Seizure direction: maintaining ketosis using the classical ketogenic diet program or not as rigorous modified Atkins diet (mad) was demonstrated successful for controlling epilepsy in both kids and adults who do not react to anti-seizure medication.

Strategies for getting to ketosis

You will find a number of ways that you may get into nutrient ketosis safely and efficiently.

- reduce daily net carbohydrate consumption to less than 20 g: though it is possible you might not have to be this rigorous, ingesting more than 20 grams of carbs daily virtually guarantees you'll achieve nutrient ketosis. What does 20 g of carbohydrate look like? Utilize our visual manual to discover, or just try our keto recipes and meal programs that restrict carbohydrates to less than 20 g daily.

- attempt intermittent fasting: going for 16-18 hours without eating can let you to get into ketosis faster quickly.

- this is simple to do by just skipping dinner or breakfast, which might feel quite natural in an appetite-suppressing keto diet.

- do not worry fat: eating lots of fat is an essential and tasty portion of ketogenic eating!

- be certain that you include a supply of healthy fat at every meal.

- cook coconut oil: along with being a pure fat which remains stable at high heat, coconut oil includes medium-chain fatty acids which could enhance ketone production and could also have other advantages.

- exercise, even if possible: throughout the transition to ketosis, you might not have sufficient energy to take part in vigorous physical activity. But simply choosing a brisk walk may allow you to get to ketosis simpler.

TYPES
of
KETOGENIC DIETS
The difference between each KETO DIET depends on carb intake

STANDARD
Ketogenic Diet
(SKD)

most common type of the
ketogenic diet

20-25g NET CARBS

TARGETED
Ketogenic Diet
(TKD)

Eat more carbs 30minutes-
1 hour before exercise
Best for athletes & body
builders

25-50g NET CARBS

CYCLICAL
Ketogenic Diet
(cKD)

Consuming Keto foods
most of the week
then eating more carbs for
a few days

20-25 NET CARBS + HIGH CARB DAYS

Restricted
Ketogenic Diet
for Therapeutic
Uses

best done under medical
supervision

below 20 NET CARBS+CALORIE RESTRICTION

A ketogenic diet is a diet that's intended to cause ketosis, the breaking down of body fat to ketones, and permit the body to run on ketones instead of glucose.

You will find a number of methods ketosis could be brought around and consequently there are a range of distinct variations of ketogenic diet.

Since the ending aim of these diets would be your samen, the various kinds of ketogenic diet generally share numerous similarities, especially in being low in carbohydrate and high in fat.

The figures in this manual are for information only and aren't an education to follow. For tips about the best way best to gather a diet, talk to a dietitian since they'll have the ability to provide you personalised advice according to your unique needs.

Standard ketogenic diet (skd)

This is a very-low carbohydrate, moderate protein and high fat dietplan. It typically contains 70 to 75 percent, 20 percent protein, and about 5 to 10 percent carbohydrates.

Concerning g daily, a standard standard ketogenic diet could be:

- 20-50g of vitamin
- 40-60g of nourishment
- no set limit for fat

Fat in the diet plan should offer nearly all calories for this for a ketogenic diet. No limit is defined as electricity requirements may vary greatly from person to person. Ketogenic diets must incorporate a strong consumption of vegetables, especially non-starchy vegetables, since these are extremely low in carbohydrate.

Standard ketogenic diets have always shown success in helping people to shed weight, improve blood sugar control and enhance cardiovascular health.

Very-low-carb ketogenic diet (vlckd)

A standard ketogenic diet plan is very-low-carb and consequently a vlckd will generally refer to some conventional ketogenic diet.

Well formulated ketogenic diet (wfkd)

The expression 'properly formulated ketogenic diet' stems from steve phinney, among the top researchers to ketogenic diets.

The wfkd follows an identical blueprint as a conventional ketogenic diet. Well devised way that the macronutrients of fat, carbohydrate and protein meet the ratios of this conventional ketogenic diet plan and so offer the best possibility of ketosis occurring.

Mct ketogenic diet

This follows the outline of regular ketogenic diet plan but includes a focus on utilizing medium chain triglycerides (mcts) to offer a lot of the fat content of your dietplan.

Mcts are located in coconut oil also can be obtained as mct oil and mct emulsion liquids. Mct ketogenic diets are used as a treatment for epilepsy since the concept is that mcts permits people to eat more protein and carbohydrate whilst maintaining in ketosis. This is only because mcts supply more ketones per g of fat compared to the long-chain triglycerides which exist in normal fat.

Notice that mcts can cause stomach upset and diarrhoea if absorbed mostly by itself. To keep this from happening, it is ideal to have meals using a balance of mcts and non-mct fat.

There's a shortage of research, however, investigating whether mcts have broader gains on weight loss or blood glucose.

Calorie-restricted ketogenic diet
A calorie-restricted ketogenic diet resembles a typical ketogenic diet except because calories are limited to some set amount.

Research shows that ketogenic diets are generally successful if calorie consumption is limited or not. This is since the satiating effect of ingesting being in ketosis will help stop overeating in itself.

Cyclical ketogenic diet (ckd)

The ckd diet, also called carbohydrate backloading, involves times where more carbohydrates are consumed, for example five ketogenic days followed by 2 high carb days.

The diet is meant for athletes that could utilize the high carb days to replenish glycogen dropped from muscles during workouts.

Targeted ketogenic diet (tkd)

The tkd is comparable to a normal ketogenic diet except carbohydrates are consumed around exercise intervals.

It's a compromise between a typical ketogenic diet plan plus also a cyclical ketogenic diet which permits you to eat carbohydrates daily that you exercise.

It's based on the notion that carbohydrate consumed before or following a physical exertion is going to be processed more efficiently, as the muscles' requirement for energy growth once we're becoming busy.

High protein ketogenic diet

This diet plan comprises more protein than a conventional ketogenic diet, using a ratio of 35 percent protein, 60 percent fat, and 5 percent carbohydrates.

Research indicates a high-protein ketogenic is effective for weight loss in people who will need to eliminate weight.

5 individuals who really can benefit from your keto diet

1. Epileptics

Initially, the primary intention of the diet was supposed to help kids who had uncontrolled seizure action, despite being treated with anti-seizure drugs. And those that are on anti-epileptic drugs may still benefit by going on the diet they might even possibly lower their dose of anti- seizure drugs with the accession of the ketogenic diet.

How can this work, exactly? Think of your thoughts as a motor engine. If it gets bombarded, seizures may occur. Whenever you have low blood sugar and consume a high-sugar meal, sugar in the kind of glucose flooding into the mind and may cause seizures. People who have a high-fat diet may experience steadier energy levels and less chance for "engine flood "

2. Type 2 diabetics (under medical supervision)

Individuals with type 2 diabetes often have hyperglycemia (elevated blood glucose levels) and insulin resistance. This induces high-circulating blood sugar which "starves" the tissues of vitality, which, in turn, generates a powerful feeling of appetite. The ketogenic diet limits blood sugar and allows the body to utilize ketones because its other fuel resource. As a result, the body obviously has lower blood sugar. After the body's sugar is decreased consistently over time, it helps cells eventually become-sensitized" into the insulin. This enables the body to utilize its energy derived from sugar.

3. Individuals that want to shed weight

For many people, the ketogenic diet is good at relieving weight reduction. When sugar is stored within the body, it is saved as a molecule known as glycogen. With every gram of glycogen that's saved, approximately 3 to 4 g of water are saved with that. It follows that if you are ingesting a carbohydrate-restricted diet, like a ketogenic one, your body utilizes its glycogen stores to keep up with your body's glucose requirements during times of fasting or even intervals without eating meals. This will result in a great number of water-weight reduction when beginning the diet.

4. Individuals that have certain kinds of cancer

The latest subject concerning the ketogenic diet is present in cancer and cancer treatments, particularly in the event of brain tumours. This can be due to a single scientist's notion that cancer cells have a huge part of sugar to provide the cells with the energy they need to develop. And we do understand that cancer cells possess an affinity for utilizing sugar, which causes a dependence on sugar as an energy supply. When ingesting a ketogenic diet, then you find yourself decreasing the quantity of blood sugar within your system, utilizing ketones instead.

This could help prevent or reduce cancer cell growth and movement.

5. Trainers

Many men and women believe which they need to have carbohydrates for an aggressive athletes, however, I am here to turn your world upside down by telling you that they are not crucial!

When you are eating mainly carbs (so 50 percent of your overall calories or more coming out of fruits, grains, and veggies), then you're considered a "sugar burner" however, if you're lean, you've got fewer sugar reserves to tap when food consumption is lean.

Meaning it to take part in a physical action, you must have a dependable supply of fuel so as to keep optimum performance and maintain with electricity requirements. A high-carbohydrate diet guarantees that sugar and carbohydrates are the dominant fuel supply for the workout. Whenever your book tank reduces, so does performance.

When you're in a condition of ketosis, however, your body isn't dependent on carbohydrates or sugar for your own cells to create and sustain vitality. When you are after a ketogenic diet and therefore are fat-adapted (meaning you've been in ketosis and keeping that condition for quite a while), you may use your ketones as fuel glucose or instead.

7 dangers of moving keto

1. The "keto influenza"

"some individuals report that if they begin ketosis, they simply feel ill, "additionally, there can at times be vomit, gastrointestinal distress, a great deal of fatigue, and lethargy." this so-called keto flu usually goes after a couple of days, she adds.

About 25 percent of individuals who attempt a keto diet encounter these signs, with fatigue being the most frequent. "that occurs because your system runs from sugar to burn energy, and it's to begin using fat," he states. "that transition is sufficient to make your body feel drowsy for a couple of days."

You may be capable to minimize the consequences of keto influenza by drinking loads of water and getting lots of sleep. Axe, that sells keto-related nutritional supplements on his web page, also recommends integrating natural energy resources to combat fatigue, such as matcha green tea, organic coffee, or adaptogenic herbs.

2. Diarrhea

If you find yourself running into the restroom more frequently while on a ketogenic diet, a fast online search will reveal to you which you are not alone. (yes, individuals are talking about keto diarrhea) this could possibly be caused by the stomach --the organ that produces bile to help break down fat from the dietfeeling "overwhelmed", states axe. Diarrhea can also be due to a lack of fiber from the keto diet says kizer, that may occur when somebody cuts back on carbohydrates (such as whole-grain pasta and bread) and does not supplement with other spicy foods, such as vegetables. It may also be due to an intolerance to milk or synthetic sweeteners--items you may be eating more of because switching into a high fat, low-carb way of life.

3. Reduced athletic performance

Some athletes vow from the ketogenic diet, not only for weight loss but also for enhanced performance in their game, too.

Participants performed on high-intensity biking and jogging jobs after four times on a ketogenic diet, in comparison to people who had spent on a diet plan. Weiss states that your system is at a more polluted condition when it is in ketosis, which might restrict its ability to perform at peak levels.

4. Ketoacidosis

For those who have kind 1 or type 2 diabetes, so you should not adhere to the keto diet if you don't have your doctor's consent and close oversight. "ketosis can really be great for men and women that have hyperglycemia difficulties, but you need to be very mindful of your blood sugar and check your sugar levels many times every day," she states.

That is because, for those who have diabetes, ketosis could cause a dangerous condition called ketoacidosis. This takes place when the body shops up too many ketones--acids generated as a by product of burning off fat --and the blood becomes overly acidic, which may harm the liver, kidneys, and brain. Left untreated, it may be deadly.

Ketoacidosis has also been reported in people with diabetes who have been after low-carb diets, though this complication is rather infrequent. Signs of ketoacidosis include a dry mouth, frequent urination, nausea, bad breath, and breathing problems; should you encounter these while after the keto diet, then check out with a physician straight away.

5. Weight recover

Since the keto diet is so restrictive, and health experts say it is not an proper strategy to follow long term. (even axe says it is best performed for 30 to 90 days, followed by a much more sustainable diet plan) however, the problem with this, is that the majority of folks will recover a great deal of the weight that they lost when they return on carbohydrates.

6. Less muscle mass, decreased metabolism

Another effect of keto-related weight changes may be a reduction of muscle mass, particularly if you're eating considerably more fat than protein. "you will eliminate weight, but it may really be a whole lot of muscle," she states, "and since muscle burns more calories than fat, which will influence your metabolism"

When a person goes off the ketogenic diet and regains a lot of the initial weight, it is frequently not in exactly the very same proportions," states kizer: rather than regaining lean muscle, you are most likely to recover fat. "now you are back to your beginning weight, but you no longer have the muscle mass to burn off the calories you just did before "that may have lasting impacts on your resting metabolic rate, and in your own weight long-term "

7. Greater risk of cardiovascular disease and diabetes
Axe states, when done correctly, the keto diet contains a lot of veggies and lean sources of animal protein. To put it differently, it is not an excuse to eat bacon and butter --though a few individuals can attempt to do precisely that.

That is why lots of health experts are worried about individuals about the ketogenic diet, in particular those who attempt it without the advice of a physician or nutritionist. High-fat diets similar to this one can increase cholesterol levels, and a few studies indicate that they raise the chance of diabetes. Some have called it a "cardiologist's nightmare"

Chapter three: Benefits of keto diet for women after 50

The unexpected advantages of low-carb diets for women over 50

Advantages of a low-carb diet for women

Both low-carb and low-carb diets may be effective for weight reduction, but, the low carb diet has some extra health benefits worth contemplating. The above-mentioned analysis analysed the effects of a low carb and low carb diet on knee pain in adults who have osteoarthritis, which affects 15% of their u.s.

After delegating subjects to a low-carb or low-carb diet, researchers discovered that the low-carb diet has been effective in reducing abdominal pain. The writers even go so far as to indicate the low carb diet may pose an alternate to pain-relieving opioids.

Additionally, low-carb diets might help improve hdl (good) cholesterol and cholesterol levels more efficiently compared to carb-heavy diets. That is probably due in part to the essence of the low carb diet -- plenty of lean proteins, healthy fats and unprocessed carbohydrates -- so that the food options are usually healthier than the conventional american diet.

Now, low-carb diets have obtained several popular kinds, for example, keto diet, the paleo diet, the Mediterranean diet. While each one of these options includes its own nuances, they are all based about reducing carbohydrate intake, while increasing healthy fat intake.

Low-carb diet basics

There is no one-size-fits-all low-carb guide, but most programs start you off on a really low-carb regime, slowly and gradually adding carbohydrates once weight is missing. Normally, low-carb diets start by limiting carbohydrates down to 20 to 60 g every day, according to the mayo clinic. The majority of the carbohydrates consumed in a low carb diet derive from vegetables such as leafy greens or berry.

After individuals lose weight, many low-carb diets gradually reintroduce carbohydrates to the meal program. Carb biking is a favourite way a lot of men and women re-integrate carbohydrates in their diet. This involves organizing your carbohydrate intake for the week according to your less or more busy days. On days you are more busy, you consume foods using a little higher carbohydrate count, whereas more sedentary times, you return to low-carb.

What to eat a low-carb diet

To maintain carbohydrates low, you are going to be eating largely carb-free proteins like beef, poultry, pork, turkey, eggs and fish. Cheese can also be full of protein, but many forms have about 1 g of carbs per oz.

But, fiber is important for women in their 40s, since it keeps blood sugar levels from spiking also quickly. A low-carb diet which makes it hard for you to receive the recommended 25 grams per day, which explains the reason why it's required to add lots of non-starchy vegetables on your own plan.

This includes alfalfa sprouts, broccoli, broccoli, bok choy, broccoli, kale, legumes, mushrooms, cucumbers, onions and lettuce. These veggies each have five grams of carbs or less per serving, based on yale medicine. As they don't spike your blood glucose, they are not contained in the"net carb" count, which describes the carbohydrate content in foods once you subtract the fiber.

Fruits can also be high in fiber, but a lot of them can also be too high in carbohydrates to match a low-carb strategy. But, pumpkin, avocados and olives every consume less than five grams of carbs per serving.

Soy foods, such as tempeh, tofu and edamame, can also be low in carbohydrates, together with three to 6 grams per serving, as well as a source of nourishment, function as a meat substitute. Whenever some soy foods are packed with fiber, minerals and vitamins, steer clear of soy isoflavone supplements and supplements containing soy protein isolate.

Ultimately, around out of your foods with carb-free fats like olive oil, ghee or avocado oil. Look out for salad dressings, as lots of them contain hidden sugars. Or look at producing your very own low-carb dressing!

Sample low-carb meal plan

If you are put on 30 grams of carbohydrates per day, for breakfast you may have a crustless frittata made with eggs, swiss cheese and sliced asparagus and onions; function it with bacon or cooked noodle. Or attempt two low-carb sandwiches made out of low-fat, almond flour-based baking combination.

For lunch, you may opt for lean chicken breast feeding with broccoli, bok choy, mung bean sprouts, sesame oil and soy sauce. You may also think about mixed greens topped sliced beef, chopped boiled egg, cucumbers, crumbled bacon and an olive oil dressing table.

Complete the day with grilled salmon with roasted brussels sprouts and turnips. A bun less hamburger topped with cheddar cheese, tomato and lettuce also creates a fantastic dinner. Serve with fresh green beans sautéed in olive oil and garlic.

Everything your hormones can do for your body on your 50s and beyond Change

of heart

The prevalence of heart attack in women increases significantly as soon as they reach menopause. Estrogen helps keep blood vessels pliable, and its decrease might explain why blood pressure and ldl, or bad cholesterol, often grow in this time period. Additionally, late peri- and postmenopause are correlated with higher fat deposits around the center, that has been associated with an increased risk (as much as 54 percent) of cardiovascular disease.

Healthful habit: blast away ab flab. The fat that forms on your center is particularly poisonous: "it generates compounds like inflammatory proteins called cytokines, which are associated with insulin resistance and type 2 diabetes in addition to heart disease. 1 possible solution would be to begin hormone treatment, but time might be crucial. "should you move on ht while you are experiencing perimenopause, it might help protect you from developing this larger belly. But should you wait till you have passed menopause, then it might be too late," if you can not take ht or want to not, concentrate on committing to regular exercise and eating a diet low in sugar and saturated fat and full of vegetables, fruits, whole grains, fish, nuts, and lean protein.

Oops, I did it again

Urinary incontinence peaks throughout menopause, with research indicating that between 30 and 40% of girls in middle age undergo some kind of urine leakage. "as estrogen levels decrease, vaginal and urinary tract tissues can weaken, which makes it more likely you are going to have episodes of incontinence," when you have put on weight, your probability of miscarriage grow, thanks to greater pressure on your bladder and surrounding tissues.

Try this: vaginal estrogen. You use itas a prescription cream, suppository, or vaginal ring-
-into your genital region to replace diminishing estrogen in these cells. "it will surely
alleviate urinary incontinence in addition to symptoms such as vaginal dryness, itching,
and irritation. Bonus: this increase of estrogen helps equilibrium amounts of vaginal
bacteria, which then retains vaginal ph (acidity) based on lowering your chance of
creating both yeast and urinary tract infections.

That's a truth!

Pelvic floor exercise helps plug flows: participants at a clinical trial reduced their
prevalence of urinary incontinence by 75 percent after only 12 weekly sessions of
physical therapy.

Not-so-tenacious

Called the sunshine vitamin as your skin synthesizes it following exposure to sun, vitamin
d acts as a hormone to help maintain strong bones and also regulate your immune system
in addition to your own muscle and nerve function. Research indicates that vitamin d
might also play a part in shielding cognition: infants 65 or older people who have been
deficient in vitamin d had a 53 percent greater chance of developing dementia; because
of the seriously paralyzed, the risk increased to 125 percent. The capability to develop
into deficient increases with age. "as you get older, your skin becomes much less effective
in utilizing the sun's beams to create vitamin d, which means that your body needs more.

Try this: think about a daily vitamin d supplement as you might be unable to get enough out of food and uv exposure alone. While the girls in their 50s and 60s get 600 ius daily, that is probably not sufficient for everybody. In a small pilot study presented at the society for endocrinology's yearly meeting last november, individuals who obtained 2,000 ius per day for 2 weeks had reduced blood pressure, lower levels of the stress hormone cortisol, as well as far better fitness functionality compared to placebo takers. But do not exceed this amount. "some research has linked elevated doses to an increased chance of developing kidney stones.

Hormones as you get older

For girls: menopause

The most common result of aging-related hormonal fluctuations is menopause. Around age 50, women's ovaries start producing decreasing quantities of progesterone and estrogen; the adrenal gland attempts to compensate by creating more follicle stimulating hormone (fsh).

While menopause is normal and happens to most girls, a few of the signs can be bothersome or even harmful. Symptoms may include these:

- Hot flashes

- Vaginal dryness and atrophy resulting in painful intercourse

- Reduced libido

- Insomnia

- Irritability/melancholy

- Osteoporosis that may increase the probability of bone fractures

- Assist with symptoms: for several decades, doctors prescribed long-term utilization of an oral estrogen/progesterone mix to relieve these symptoms.

However, a study in the early 2000s demonstrated that those taking hormone replacement therapy had a greater chance of stroke, cardiovascular disorder, breast cancer and blood clots.

Present guidelines imply that it is fine to take progesterone and estrogen for a brief period to assist with the transition to menopause and there are ongoing research investigating the efficacy and safety of various progesterone and estrogen formulas that may possibly be utilized for longer amounts of time.

Alternative therapies, for example bioidentical hormones generated from animal or plant sources, have not yet been thoroughly assessed for safety and efficacy.

So for today, try listed below:

Non-hormonal drugs can handle hot flashes

Topical herbal lotion used vaginally can assist with painful sex.

Leading a healthy lifestyle that incorporates a balanced diet, regular physical activity and anxiety management helps relieve many symptoms of menopause.

It is also important for women to have regular bone-density screenings starting at age 65 to capture osteoporosis early.

Ketogenic diet for weight loss

The ketogenic or "keto" diet is a non-prescription, fat-rich eating program that's been used for many years to treat certain health problems. From the 19th century, the ketogenic diet has been commonly utilized to help control diabetes. In 1920 it had been released as an effective remedy for epilepsy in children in which medication was unsuccessful. The ketogenic diet has also been analyzed and used in carefully tracked settings for diabetes, cancer, polycystic ovary syndrome, and alzheimer's disease.

But this diet is gaining substantial attention as a possible weight-loss strategy on account of the low-carb diet fad, which began in the 1970s using the Atkins diet plan (a very low fat, high- protein diet plan, which has been a commercial success and popularized low-carb diets to some other level). Now, other low carb diets such as the paleo, south beach, and dukan diets are high in protein but moderate in fat loss. By comparison, the ketogenic diet is unique because of its exceptionally high-fat content, generally 70% to 80%, although with just a moderate consumption of protein.

How it works

The assumption of the ketogenic diet for weight reduction is that in case you deprive the body of sugar --the principal source of energy to most cells within the body, that can be acquired by eating carbohydrate foods--an alternate fuel known as ketones is generated from stored fat (consequently, the expression"keto"-genic). The mind needs the maximum glucose in a continuous source, about 120 g each day, since it cannot store glucose. During fasting, or if very little carbohydrate is consumed, the body pulls stored sugar in the liver and briefly breaks down muscle to release sugar. If it lasts for 3-4 times and saved sugar is totally depleted, blood levels of a hormone known as insulin reduction, and the body starts to utilize fat as its main fuel. The liver also produces ketone bodies from fat, which may be utilised in the absence of sugar.

When ketone bodies collect in the bloodstream, this is known as ketosis. Healthy people naturally experience moderate ketosis during times of fasting (e.g., sleeping immediately) and quite strenuous exercise. Proponents of this ketogenic diet condition that when the diet is closely followed, blood levels of ketones shouldn't reach a damaging amount (called "ketoacidosis") since the mind will use ketones for fuel, and wholesome people will normally generate enough insulin to stop excess ketones from forming. How soon ketosis occurs and the amount of ketone bodies which collect in the bloodstream is varying from person to person and depends upon factors like body fat percent and resting metabolic rate.

The diet plan

There's not one "standard" ketogenic diet with a particular proportion of macronutrients (carbs, protein, fat). The ketogenic diet generally reduces overall carbohydrate consumption to less than 50 grams a day--less than the amount found at a moderate plain bagel--also may be as low as 20 grams each day. Normally, popular ketogenic sources imply an average of 70-80percent fat out of total daily calories, 5-10% carb, and 10-20% protein. To get a 2000-calorie daily diet, that equates to approximately 165 g fat, 40 g carbohydrate, and 75 g protein. The protein level onto the ketogenic diet is stored moderate in contrast with other low carb diets, because eating too much protein may prevent ketosis. The amino acids in protein could be converted into sugar, therefore a ketogenic diet stipulates enough protein to maintain lean body mass such as muscle, but which will still result in ketosis.

Many variations of ketogenic diets exist, but ban carb-rich foods. Some of those foods could be evident: starches from refined and whole grains such as cereals, breads, rice, pasta, and biscuits; berries, corn, and other starchy veggies; and fruit juices. Some which might not be quite as apparent are beans, legumes, and fruits. Many ketogenic programs make it possible for foods high in saturated fat, such as fatty cuts of meat, processed meats, lard, and butter, in addition to sources of unsaturated fats, like nuts, seeds, avocados, plant oils, and fatty fish. Based upon your source of advice, ketogenic food lists can vary and also battle.

Keto diet into withered bones

Physicians and researchers across areas have decried the keto diet, particularly over the last couple of decades, because its popularity as a fast method to eliminate weight surged. Observing the diet properly involves getting up to 90 percent of a person's daily calories in fats, which is intended to send the body to some semi-starvation condition called "ketosis." the notion is that, while in ketosis, ketoers burn reserved fat stores for energy, instead of crying through easily available carbohydrates. That may (and can) help people shed weight, but it's also extremely unsustainable, and seems to develop with a complete mess of wellness problems.

The only known clinical usage for keto is treating epilepsy in children; it has been helpful for helping regulate glucose levels in people with diabetes. But simply because a diet plan is doctor- approved for certain situations does not mean it is a great idea to use it "off-label" for fat reduction without doctor advice. If your aim is to lose fat, then there are loads of different methods to do this without rotting body systems that are crucial, and virtually all them are far less bothersome.

Could ingesting a keto or lchf diet injury bone health?

Keto diet increased markers of bone breakdown and decreased markers of bone formation. After individuals in the keto group included carbohydrates back to their own diet, a few of those markers recovered, whereas the others stayed changed. The authors reasoned that keto diets may have harmful effects on bone health and further long-term studies are justified.

This may sound about to those people who follow a keto or even lchf manner of eating. But, there are a number of things to think about here.

First, what exactly do the fluctuations in these markers imply for bone health in the long run? We really do not understand. Might they've improved in their own following a span of keto- adaptation, which may take weeks? A research lasting less than 4 months only can not predict what may happen months or years afterwards. We would want dexa scans and other information to evaluate if there was any link between eating low carb and bone loss or other issues.

Secondly, this was an analysis of elite athletes, so answers may differ among individuals people who fall out of this category.

Last, the writers' recommendation for additional research on the long-term ramifications of low carb diets on bone health appear to create sense. However there are already a few more high blood trials using dexa scans along with other information that show no harmful effects of ketogenic diets on bones.

Keto diet can protect against cognitive decline

Ketogenic, or keto, diets are low carb and fat-rich, and several men and women who follow these regimens take action to lose extra weight. But a keto diet can bring other advantages, too.

Specifically, it might help keep the mind healthy and youthful, as new study in mice appears to suggest.

This type of diet is supposed to activate ketosis, and it can be a metabolic process whereby the body breaks down protein and fat and transforms them to energy, resulting in weight loss.

Apart from triggering weight reduction, a keto diet might also bring additional health advantages, as studies have recently indicated. As an example, one such study contended that keto diets might lower the unwanted effects of cancer treatments.

Now, assessing evidence indicating that keto diets can also help stave off cognitive decline.

The scientists conducted two studies, both in mice. The findings suggest that keto-type diets may shield neurovascular function, in addition to metabolic function, generally, which might assist the creatures maintain healthy cognitive functioning.

Keto diet clears outside beta-amyloid

The initial study, whose results appear in the journal scientific reports, appeared at the ramifications of a keto diet on neurovascular function, including motor and sensory capabilities, in addition to flow.

The group worked with two groups of mice per day, all which were obsolete 12-14 weeks. The animals received either a ketogenic diet plan or a normal diet for 16 weeks.

Following this interval, the scientists discovered that the mice which had followed the keto regimen hadn't only improved blood circulation to the brain, but also better bacterial balance in the intestine, in addition to lower blood sugar (sugar), and reduced body fat.

Moreover, and most of all, the keto diet seemed to raise the clearance of beta-amyloid protein within the mind -- the "building blocks" that, in Alzheimer's, stay together, forming toxic plaques that interfere with neuronal signalling.

"neurovascular ethics, such as cerebral blood circulation and adrenal barrier function, plays a significant role in cognitive capability.

"recent science has implied that neurovascular integrity may be modulated by the bacteria in the intestine, "therefore we set out to check if the ketogenic diet improved brain vascular functioning and decreased neurodegeneration danger in young wholesome mice"

Using diet to mitigate risk' of dementia

"while diet alterations, the ketogenic diet, in particular, has shown effectiveness in treating specific ailments, we opted to test healthy young mice, with diet as a possible preventative step," she further clarifies.

"we're thrilled to find out that we could really be in a position to use diet to mitigate risk for Alzheimer's disease"

Even though it is unsure what mechanisms are put in movement by the keto diet within this circumstance, lin supposes that the protective effects to the mind could be due the fact that this routine basically inhibits a nutrient detector called mechanistic target of rapamycin (mtor).

Past research has implied that mtor signalling has a significant effect on aging procedures along with also an individual's lifespan.

It's also potential to target mtor through caloric restriction -- a dietary plan that, as its name implies, limits the consumption of carbs -- or simply by simply administering the enzyme rapamycin.

'Tremendous consequences for clinical trials'

From the next research -- whose findings that they printed in the journal frontiers in aging neuroscience -- that the researchers examined the brains of mice that received one of three interventions: a dose of rapamycin, vulnerability to the keto diet, or easy caloric restriction.

In cases like this, the researchers worked together with both aging and young animals to comprehend the effects of the interventions on cognitive function.

"our previous work already demonstrated the favorable impact rapamycin and caloric restriction needed on neurovascular function,: "we theorized that neuroimaging might permit us to find those changes in the brain"

The investigators' data suggested that caloric restriction could enhance neurovascular and metabolic function in aging mice, thus shielding their mind health.

Inside this mouse version neurovascular and metabolic function seems to work better than in mice whose diets weren't restricted.

Desire a better night's sleep? The keto diet may help

"it is not rare to hear people report sleeping difficulties when they begin a ketogenic diet," notes Michael j. Breas, phd, a clinical psychologist with a specialization in sleep disorders. "a huge decrease in carbohydrate intake together with considerable increase to fat consumption -- that occurs on a keto diet can create changes to sleep patterns. All these macronutrients have different consequences in the human body and may impact sleep in different ways."

Just a little number of research have carefully analyzed how keto diets influence sleep," states breus. However, what they reveal so much is that "that exact low carb, high-fat diet can offer advantages for sleep, either through weight reduction and other pathways"

For example, nutrients, a bunch of Columbian scientists discovered a very low carb keto diet significantly reduced daytime sleepiness at a group of obese individuals.

Six morbidly obese adolescents who spent 4 weeks on a keto diet. While all revealed lean rem (dreaming) sleep and excess slow-wave (deep) sleep at the start of the experimentation, the opposite was true in the conclusion.

A different Swedish research found that kids who have hard-to-treat epilepsy who followed a keto diet trusted source slept better, experienced greater rem sleep, also felt less tired throughout the daytime -- all of which enhanced their overall wellbeing.

1 theory as to what is happening: ketogenic diets might have an impact on a brain chemical called adenosine that is significant to sleep management, breus states.

"adenosine assembles up from the body through the day and leads to our sense less alert and wakeful as the afternoon continues, eventually helping promote deeper slow-wave sleep during the night," explains breus. "studies reveal a ketogenic diet boosts adenosine action within the human body, helping to relax the nervous system, in addition to reducing pain trusted supply and inflammation all of that may help improve sleep"

However, more research has to be carried out.

Keto insomnia

Better sleep does not arrive overnight, however.

During her first month about the keto diet, keiwana eaton fell 25 lbs... Yet discovered herself awake and full of energy.

"i am normally annoyed by 9 pm -- 10 if there is a fantastic picture on -- but not later than this," states that the opelika, alabama resident.

"keto insomnia" is an actual, albeit frequently short-lived, occurrence for a number of people. And like keto's capability to assist sleep, its causes continue to be sussed out.

Low levels of serotonin and endorphins, endorphins that assist with sleep, in addition to greater than normal energy levels, can be partially to blame. "[you are] not eating several carbohydrates so that you do not possess the l-tryptophan [an amino acid present in foods] which allegedly helps with raising melatonin and serotonin..

And, "when folks do not have energy slumps anymore -- yet another advantage of keto -- reaching for a three pm coffee will stop, which could also help sleep grade boost," Sanfilippo adds.

Is your keto diet right for you? Getty images

However keto is a daily diet, not a sleeping aid

Just because you're on the lookout for much better shut-eye does not mean that you should jump to the keto bandwagon. (regardless of how much you really adore the thought of cheese at each meal)

Check with your doctor first to determine whether this eating program's a fantastic match for you. Meanwhile, to have a better night's rest, you are able to:

- Cut candy. Try new fruit instead. The more sugar you consume throughout the day, the more frequently you will wake throughout the night-time.
- Proceed at Starbucks. "1 cup of coffee in the morning may negatively impact sleep during the night. Switch to half-caf for each week, then finally to decaf, then no coffee in any way, and "you will probably find a noticeable improvement in sleep quality," she states.
- Ditch that the booze. "alcohol is a touchy issue for those who lean on it to unwind. But, removing your everyday beverage can help you sleep more soundly and enhance your energy the following day, also.
- Up your own exercise. "adding 30 to 60 minutes of whatever from walking into weight lifting to yoga to high-intensity exercise will help improve your sleep quality.

KETO Food Pyramid

Healthy foods to boost your energy to a ketogenic diet

Low carb keto energy boosters Oily fish

Oily fish, such as salmon, mackerel, trout, mackerel and sardines, is full of fatty acids and b vitamins. All these are therefore a fantastic food to add in a keto diet.

One serving of fatty fish will provide you your preferred daily dose of vitamin b12 and is an superb source of omega-3 fatty acids.

Studies have indicated that omega-3 fatty acids can decrease inflammation within the body. This is important because inflammation may lead to fatigue.

Vitamin b12 and folic acid help create red blood cells, which assists iron function better within the body. Possessing optimum levels of iron in the bloodstream may also decrease fatigue and improve energy levels.

Take a browse of those keto fish recipes in case you're searching for keto meal ideas which have fatty fish.

Eggs

Eggs could be great included in a meal or as a snack, as they will not offer you spikes in blood glucose and energy crashes which high-carb foods may lead to during digestion.

Eggs are full of protein and therefore are a sustained energy supply which can get you through the next meal.

The b vitamins in eggs assist enzymes break down food for energy and also the critical amino acid leucine helps to consume glucose from the blood. Leucine also arouses energy generation in cells by increasing the breakdown of fat required within a keto diet.

In summary, eggs are equally tasty, filling and nutritious. They may be enjoyed by themselves or contained in several distinct kinds of keto recipes and meals.

Seeds

Seeds are an excellent source of fiber, so the nutrients from the food will be digested more slowly. This also contributes to a constant release of energy, assisting you maintain your energy levels between meals, which can be important whether you are looking for a low carb ketogenic diet plan.

Chia seeds and flaxseeds can provide you an energy boost and may be added to salads, mixed into smoothies or built into healthful multiseed keto crackers.

All these kinds of seeds are abundant in plant-based omega-3 fatty acids, which makes them a suitable energy source for vegans, and may also decrease inflammation and tiredness. Chia and flax seeds also contain a lot more omega-3 compared to omega-6 fatty acids, whereas the reverse is true of many other kinds of seeds.

This is critical to keep in mind, because though omega-6 is a essential fatty acid your body requires in healthy amounts, many people currently have a lot of in their everyday diet. It is therefore best to eat seeds in moderation, and also adhere to seeds which are reduced in omega-6.

As the essential fatty acids in seeds are fermented, making them a suitable energy source for vegans. As seeds are also a fantastic source of protein, making them an important element in a ketogenic diet.

Chia seeds may be added to smoothies or built into multiseed crackers Nuts
When you initially begin a ketogenic diet, the absence of carbohydrates may depart from your energy amounts aggressively, particularly between meals. It is therefore important to maintain a healthy, high energy, low-fat ketogenic snacks available.

Nuts for example almonds, walnuts, brazil nuts, macadamia nuts and cashews are packed with nutrients and are great as a snack in case you are hungry between meals and require an energy increase.

They're also another fantastic source of healthful omega-3 and omega-6 fatty acids, in addition to antioxidants which could boost energy levels by assisting to reduce inflammation within the body.

Like nuts, seeds contain fiber, boosting a gradual and sustained release of energy when you want it. They also contain minerals and vitamins like b vitamins, vitamin e, iron and manganese, which can help boost energy generation and reduce fatigue.

Macadamia nuts may be great healthy high-fat energy bites around the keto diet Nut butters
That is just another means of eating nuts, and it delivers the exact same health and vitality benefits. Just be certain that you check the components if you are purchasing from a shop rather than creating your own. Many manufacturers include a great deal of sugar, salt, unhealthy additives and fats for their nut butter, and that you are going to wish to prevent.

If you would like to reduce your carbohydrate intake as part of your ketogenic dietplan, macadamia nuts are a decrease carbohydrate nut. They also possess a ideal omega-3 into omega- 6 fatty acid percentage, and that means that you will not be overdoing it using all the omega-6 fatty acids. Consider creating your own macadamia nut butter by simply adding a few to a food processor with a few cashews, and coconut mct oil to get an excess energy boost.

If you want peanut butter, the most economical alternative is to create your own homemade peanut butter.

Now, you might be wondering: just how can you consume nut butter in case you can not distribute it onto a piece of bread (that can be high in carbohydrates and aren't acceptable to get a keto diet)? Simple answer - bake some bread from your nut butter!

Here's a straightforward recipe you can try in your home - keto peanut butter bread - and you may also try creating your own multiseed keto crackers.

Homemade nut butter (photo: march verch, cc from 2.0) Grass fed butter
Butter is high in calories and fat and consequently a useful high energy food to have in your keto diet plan. But, grass-fed butter might be more healthy, as it includes a greater percentage of healthful unsaturated omega-3 fatty acids.

Avocado

Avocados are a fantastic supply of healthy monounsaturated fats and polyunsaturated fatty acids and fiber. These could be saved in the human body and utilized as a supply of vitality, and aid the absorption of nourishment.

80 percent of the avocado's carbohydrate content is composed of fiber, which helps regulate energy levels, as nourishment is consumed slowly.

The b vitamins in avocados also help preserve the normal function of cells' mitochondria, where cells receive their energy.

Avocados are good to eat by themselves, or can be made to a tasty guacamole dip or added to salads. If you would like to create your smoothies creamier without including a banana, avocado is also a excellent option.

A high protein, low carb smoothie

Smoothies are a fantastic keto or paleo energy beverage when you're on the lookout for something yummy to fill up you fast and provide you that boost you want.

Our primal one chocolate powder is perfect if you are craving a chocolate milkshake with no carbohydrates. The premium excellent whey protein will help to preserve muscle and also the medium chain triglycerides (mct - healthful fatty acids) we have added to it provide an instant yet slow release of energy. Additionally, we have added organic maca origin into the powder, which study has demonstrated may improve endurance. Mix it up with some water and almond milk and revel in a tasty high energy low-carb smoothie.

Alternatively, you may earn a coconut smoothie with coconut milk. Add some stevia for sweetness and a number of our primal energy coconut mct oil (read about mct oil under) for an excess energy boost. Ensure it is a cinnamon smoothie by incorporating 1/2 tsp of cinnamon and a few chia seeds for additional fiber and omega-3 fatty acids.

Should you prefer a fruity flavour, strawberries, raspberries and blackberries include fewer carbohydrates than other fruits. You might even try our low carb bitter lemon flavoured adapt advanced pre workout drink, that will leave you feeling energized before a hectic day.

Extra virgin olive oil

Olive oil is just one of the principles of the mediterranean diet, widely thought to be why most folks in southern europe dwell more.

One of those advantages of olive oil is the oleic acid within it's a satiating effect. It slows down the absorption of nutrients within the human body in order that energy is going to be released more slowly. This usually means you are going to feel good for longer and will not feel the need to snack on snacks between meals.

So although olive petroleum is full of calories, this should not set you off, since you'll be tempted to snack on unhealthy foods during the day.

Mct oil

Mct stands for medium chain triglycerides, a kind of fat that occurs naturally from coconut oil. Mct oil is readily absorbed by the human body and are not processed through the lymphatic system; they're in reality transported right to the liver to be broken down. This creates ketones, which your muscles and other cells use for fuel rather than sugar to get an immediate and continuous release of energy. This will be handy for your muscles if you are arranging a work out, or to your mind if you want an excess increase of concentration on the job.

Our primal energy mct c8 oil is among the maximum quality and may be added to salad dressings, sauces and your morning coffee when you want a quick, healthful energy boost.

Fatty cuts of red black and meat poultry meat

If you are searching for ideas to the high fat low carbohydrate foods, unprocessed poultry and meat (chicken, turkey, duck) are a few of the basic foods of a ketogenic diet they contain no carbohydrates and are high in protein and fat. The protein can help you to maintain and build muscles (if you are working out) on a keto diet, and the fat is broken down to create energy.

Grass-fed meat is preferable over grain-fed meat, even if it is possible to get it. This is because it's more nutritious, containing higher amounts of antioxidants, omega-3 fatty acids and conjugated linoleic acid (important for cell metabolism).

The way low-carb and ketogenic diets supply energy for your brain
Low-carb diets have a fascinating method of providing your mind with energy through procedures called ketogenesis and gluconeoegenesis.

Ketogenesis

Glucose, the sugar within your bloodstream, is normally the brain's most important fuel. Unlike muscle, your mind can not use fat as a fuel source.

However, the brain may use ketones. Your liver produces ketones from fatty acids when insulin and glucose levels are reduced.

Ketones are actually produced in tiny quantities whenever you like several hours without eating, like following a complete night's sleep.

However, the liver increases its own production of ketones even farther during fasting or whenever carbohydrate intake drops under 50 g every day.

When carbohydrates are eliminated or diminished, ketones can supply around 70 percent of their brain's energy requirements.

Gluconeogenesis

Although most of the mind may use ketones, you will find parts that need glucose to operate. On a very-low-carb diet, a number of the glucose can be provided by the little number of carbs consumed.

The remainder comes from a procedure on your body known as gluconeogenesis, so"producing new glucose" within this procedure, the liver generates glucose to the brain to utilize. It generates the sugar utilizing amino acids, the building blocks of protein.

The liver can make sugar from glycerol. This is actually the backbone which links fatty acids collectively in triglycerides, the human body's storage form of fat.

Due to gluconeogenesis, the parts of the mind which require glucose get a continuous supply, even if your carbohydrate intake is extremely low.

Low-carb/ketogenic foods and alzheimer's disease

Although few formal studies have been completed, it seems that low-carb and ketogenic diets can be helpful for individuals with alzheimer's disease.

Alzheimer's disorder is the most common type of dementia. It is a progressive disease in which the mind develops plaques and tangles which cause memory loss.

Many researchers consider it needs to be considered"type 3" diabetes since the brain's cells become insulin resistant and also are not able to use glucose properly, resulting in inflammation.

Actually, metabolic syndrome, also a stepping stone in type 2 diabetes, also raises the probability of developing alzheimer's disease.

Pros report this alzheimer's disease shares certain features with epilepsy, such as brain excitability which contributes to seizures.

In 1 study of 152 individuals with alzheimer's disease, individuals that obtained an mct supplement for 90 days had considerably higher ketone rates and a substantial improvement in brain function in contrast to a control group.

Animal research also imply a ketogenic diet may be an efficient method to fuel a mind affected by alzheimer's disease.

Much like epilepsy, researchers are not sure of the specific mechanism behind these possible gains against alzheimer's disease.

1 theory is that ketones protect brain cells by decreasing reactive oxygen species, which are byproducts of metabolism that may lead to inflammation.

Low-carb/ketogenic foods and alzheimer's disease

Although few formal studies have been completed, it seems that low-carb and ketogenic diets can be helpful for individuals with alzheimer's disease.

Alzheimer's disorder is the most common type of dementia. It is a progressive disease in which the brain develops plaques and tangles which cause memory loss.

Many researchers think it ought to be considered"type 3" diabetes since the brain's cells become insulin resistant and also cannot use glucose properly, resulting in inflammation (26trusted supply, 27trusted supply, 28trusted source).

In reality, metabolic infection, a stepping stone in type 2 diabetes, also raises the probability of developing alzheimer's disease (28trusted supply, 29trusted source).

Pros report this alzheimer's disease shares certain features with epilepsy, such as brain excitability which contributes to seizures (30trusted source, 31trusted source).

In 1 study of 152 individuals with alzheimer's disease, individuals who obtained an mct supplement for 90 days had considerably higher ketone levels and a substantial improvement in brain function in contrast to a control group (32trusted source).

Animal research also imply a ketogenic diet may be an efficient method to fuel a mind affected by alzheimer's (27trusted supply, 33trusted source).

Much like epilepsy, researchers are not sure of the specific mechanism behind these possible gains against alzheimer's disease.

1 theory is that ketones protect brain cells by decreasing reactive oxygen species, which are byproducts of metabolism that may lead to inflammation.

Additional benefits for your brain

Though these have not been analyzed too much, low-carb and ketogenic diets might have other advantages for the mind:

- Performance: older adults at risk of alzheimer's disease have demonstrated improvement in memory following a very-low-carb diet for 2 weeks.
- Brain role: feeding obese and older rats that a ketogenic diet contributes to enhanced brain function.
- Congenital hyperinsulinism: this illness causes hypoglycemia and may result in

brain damage. Congenital hyperinsulinism was successfully treated using a ketogenic diet.

- Migraine headaches: researchers report low-carb or ketogenic diets might offer relief to migraine sufferers

- Parkinson's disease: in a small, uncontrolled study, five out of seven individuals who have parkinson's disease that finished a four-week ketogenic diet experienced a 43% increase in self-reported symptoms.

- Traumatic brain injury: patients with acute head trauma who were fed with a carb-free formulation could receive nourishment whilst preventing high blood glucose, which may interfere with healing.

Blood sugar level ranges

Recognizing blood sugar levels can be an integral portion of diabetes self-management.

This page says 'ordinary' blood glucose ranges and blood glucose levels for adults and children with type 1 diabetes, type two diabetes and blood glucose ranges to ascertain individuals with diabetes.

If a individual with diabetes includes a meter, test strips and is analyzing, it is important to be aware of what the blood sugar level implies.

Recommended blood glucose levels possess a level of interpretation for every single person and you need to discuss this with your health care team.

Additionally, women might be put goal glucose levels during pregnancy.

The next ranges are guidelines offered by the national institute for clinical excellence (nice) but every person's target range ought to be consented by their physician or diabetic adviser.

Recommended target blood sugar level ranges

The nice recommended target blood sugar levels are mentioned below for adults who have type 1 diabetes, type two diabetes and children with type 1 diabetes.

Additionally, the international diabetes federation's goal ranges for individuals without diabetes is said. The table offers overall advice. A single goal determined by your health care team is the one which you should plan for.

Regular and diabetic blood glucose ranges

For most of healthy people, normal glucose levels are as follows:

Between 4.0 to 5.4 mmol/l (72 to 99 mg/dl) when fasting [361] As much as 7.8 mmol/l (140 mg/dl) two hours after ingestion

For individuals with diabetes, blood glucose level goals are as follows:

Before foods: 4 to 7 mmol/l for individuals with type 1 or type 2 diabetes
After foods: below 9 mmol/l for those who have type 1 diabetes and below 8.5mmol/l

for individuals with type two diabetes.

Chapter four Recipes

Breakfast recipes

Keto shepherd's pie

Yields: 4 - 6 servings

***Prep time:** 0 hours 15 mins*

***Total time:** 0 hours 50 mins*

Ingredients

- ✓ 1 medium head cauliflower, cut into florets (about 6 cups) 4 ounces. Lotion cheese, softened
- ✓ 1/4 c. Heavy lotion
- ✓ 1 - 1/2 c. Shredded cheddar, split
- ✓ 2 green onions, thinly sliced Kosher salt
- ✓ Freshly ground black pepper
- ✓ 1 tablespoon. Extra-virgin olive oil 1 small yellow chopped
- ✓ 1 medium carrot, peeled and chopped 1 teaspoon garlic, minced
- ✓ 1 tablespoon. Tomato glue 1 pounds. Ground beef
- ✓ 1/2 c. Low-sodium beef broth

Instructions

1. Preheat oven to 400°. Bring a large pot of salted water to a boil. Add cauliflower florets and cook till tender, 10 minutes. Drain well, pressing paper towels or a clean dish towel to remove as much excess water as you can.
2. Return cauliflower to pot and add cream cheese. Use a potato masher to mash cauliflower till smooth. Add heavy cream, 1 cup cheddar, and half the green onions and stir to blend. Season well with pepper and salt.

3. Within an oven-safe skillet over moderate heat, heat oil. Add carrots and onion and cook until tender, 5 minutes. Add garlic and cook until fragrant, 1 minute longer. Add tomato paste and stir to coat veggies. Add ground beef to skillet and with a wooden spoon to break up meat, cook until no longer pink, 6 minutes. Season with pepper and salt. Add broth and simmer 2 minutes.

4. Top skillet with cauliflower mash, then top with remaining 1/2 cup of cheddar. Bake until top is golden and cheese is melty, 20 minutes.

5. Shirt with more green onions to serve.

Carne asada fries

Yields: *4 - 6 servings*

Prep time: *0 hours 25 mins*

Total time: *1 hour 0 mins*

Ingredients

- ✓ For the seasoning mix 2 tsp. Garlic powder
- ✓ 1 1/2 tsp. Onion powder 1 1/2 tsp. Paprika
- ✓ 1 tsp. Lately ground pepper 1/4 tsp. Cayenne
- ✓ For those fries and beef
- ✓ 1 (1-lb.) Bundle frozen fries
- ✓ 12 oz. Flank beef, sliced into 5" segments 1 tablespoon. Vegetable petroleum Kosher salt
- ✓ For your cheese sauce 3 tablespoons. Butter
- ✓ 3 tablespoons. All-purpose flour 1 c. Whole milk
- ✓ 2 c. Shredded cheddar Kosher salt
- ✓ For serving 2 avocados
- ✓ 1 1/2 tbsp. Lime juice Kosher salt
- ✓ 1 medium tomato, diced
- ✓ 1 small yellow onion, finely diced 1/4 c. Sour cream

Instructions

Create the seasoning blend: mix all ingredients in a small bowl.

Make hamburgers and beef: preheat oven to 425°. On a large baking sheet, then bake french fries in one layer in accordance with package directions. Season with salt to flavor instantly when they're baked.

Meanwhile, rub beef with vegetable oil and season with 1 1/2 tsp salt and one tbsp seasoning mixture. Heat a medium cast iron skillet over medium-high warmth. Add beef and cook flipping once, until a heavy golden crust forms on either side of the beef, about 5 minutes complete. Let meat rest 10 minutes before slicing into 1" cubes.

Make cheese sauce: in a medium saucepan over moderate heat, melt butter. Add flour and cook until just golden, 1 to 2 minutes longer. Add milk and bring to a simmer, then whisk in cheese and allow simmer, 3 to 5 minutes longer.

Construct: in a little bow, mash salmon with lime juice and one tsp seasoning mixture, and season with salt. Leading fries with cheese sauce, chopped beef, mashed avocado, tomato, onion, and a dollop of sour cream. Sprinkle on remaining seasoning mixture and serve immediately.

Pulled pork nachos

Ingredients

- ✓ 1 1/2 pounds. Ready pulled pork 1/4 c. Barbecue sauce
- ✓ 1 (13-oz.) Bag corn chips

- ✓ 4 c. Shredded monterey jack

- ✓ 1 c. Sliced pickled jalapeños, emptied 1/4 red onion, finely chopped
- ✓ 1 avocado, halved and pitted Juice of 1/2 lime

✓ 1/4 c. Freshly chopped cilantro leaves, plus more for garnish Kosher salt

✓ Freshly ground black pepper Sour cream, for serving

Instructions

Preheat oven to 375° and line a large baking sheet with aluminum foil. In a large bowl combine pulled pork and barbecue sauce.

Spread an even layer of chips on the baking sheet, then high with 1/3 of those peppers, cheese, and pulled pork. Top with more chips and yet another 1/3 of peppers, cheese, and pork. Finish with one final layer of fries and the rest of the cheese, peppers, and pork.

Bake until cheese is melty and chips have crisped marginally, 10 seconds.

Meanwhile, in a medium bowl, mash avocado with lime juice and cilantro. Season with pepper and salt.

When nachos are finished baking, dollop with guacamole and sour cream. Drink immediately.

Buffalo chicken monkey bread

Yields: *10 servings*

Prep time: *0 hours 20 mins*

Total time: *1 hour 40 mins*

Ingredients

- ✓ Cooking spray

- ✓ Two (16.3-oz.) Cans biscuit dough 2 c. Shredded cooked chicken
- ✓ c. Buffalo sauce, split 2 c. Shredded mozzarella

✓ 1/2 c. Freshly grated parmesan

✓ thinly sliced green onions, and more for garnish Ranch dressing, for serving

Instructions

Preheat oven to 350° and dirt a large bundt pan with cooking spray. Cut each biscuit into quarters.

In a medium bowl, toss chicken and 3/4 cup buffalo sauce together. Pour remaining 1/4 cup sauce into prepared bundt pan.

Set about a third of those biscuit quarters.

Layer with half the chicken, mozzarella, parmesan, and green onions.

Top with another third of those snacks and staying chicken, mozzarella, parmesan, and green onions. Top with remaining biscuits. Bake until golden and melty, 1 hour.

Cover with foil if top begins to get too dim.

Let cool for 10 minutes, then turn onto a serving dish. Drizzle with top and ranch with more green onions.

Blt egglets

Yields: *6 servings*

Prep time: *0 hours 25 mins*

Total time: *0 hours 35 mins*

Ingredients

- ✓ 6 large eggs

- ✓ 2 pieces thick-cut bacon, cut into quarters 1/4 c. Mayonnaise

- ✓ 1 tablespoon. Lately chopped chives 1 tsp. Red wine vinegar

- ✓ 1 tsp. Hot sauce (like cholula) Kosher salt
- ✓ Freshly ground black pepper 1/2 c. Quartered grape tomatoes 1/2 c. Shredded romaine lettuce

Instructions

Put eggs in a large pot and cover by an inch of cold water. Put pot on stove and bring to a boil. Instantly turn heat off and cover pot. Let sit for 11 minutes. Meanwhile, prepare a medium bowl of ice cold water. When 11 minutes is up, drain eggs and submerge in ice cold water.

Meanwhile, heat a large skillet over moderate heat. Add bacon and cook until crispy, about 4 minutes each side. Remove from pan and drain on a paper towellined plate. In a medium bowlwhisk to combine mayo, chives, red wine vinegar, and hot sauce. Season with pepper and salt.

Peel and halve eggs. Spread mayo mixture on the cut side of a single egg. Top with tomatoes, bacon, and lettuce, then top with other half egg. Season with pepper and salt and serve.

Lunch recipes

Reverse sear steak

Yields: *2 servings*

Prep time: *0 hours 20 mins*

Total time: *1 hour 20 mins*

Ingredients

- ✓ 2"-thick rib eye beef (about 14 oz.) Kosher salt
- ✓ Freshly ground black pepper Canola oil
- ✓ tablespoons. Butter
- ✓ Cloves garlic, crushed 2
- ✓ Sprigs rosemary Flaky sea salt

Instructions

Preheat oven to 225°. Season beef generously with pepper and salt. Transfer beef to a wire rack set at a sheet and simmer for 50 to 55 minutes, until internal temperatures of beef is 125° for medium rare. (if you want a more well done beef, correct time as necessary for fever.)

In a moderate cast iron skillet medium-high, heat until nearly smoking. Add beef and cook flipping once, until a heavy golden crust starts to form on cither side of the steak, about 1 minute per side.

Reduce heat to medium and add butter, garlic, and rosemary to the pan. With a kitchen towel, then carefully hold the skillet and lean towards you to ensure the melting butter creates a pool in the bottom of the skillet. With a spoon, always baste butter on beef to make a deeper gold crust. Be certain the garlic and rosemary have been submerged in the butter; this is going to assist their flavors meld together. If the beef has some excess fat round the sides, then use tongs to consume the beef on its own side and leave the fat out.

Transfer beef onto a cutting board and let rest about 10 minutes to lock in the juices. Slice on a prejudice against the grain, scatter with flaky salt and more pepper.

Ham egg & cheese roll-ups

Cal/serv: *410*

Yields: *10*

Prep time: *0 hours 15 mins*

Total time: *0 hours 35 mins*

Ingredients

- ✓ 10 large eggs

- ✓ 2 tsp. Garlic powder Kosher salt
- ✓ Freshly ground black pepper 2 tablespoons. Butter
- ✓ 1/2 c. Shredded cheddar 1 c. Baby spinach
- ✓ c. Chopped berries 20 slices ham

Instructions

Heat broiler. In a big bowl, crack eggs. Whisk with garlic powder and season with pepper and salt.

In a large nonstick skillet over moderate heat, melt butter. Add eggs and scramble, stirring occasionally, 3 minutes. Stir in cheddar until melted, then stir in baby spinach and berries until blended.

On a cutting board, place two pieces of ham. Top with a huge spoonful of scrambled eggs and roll up. Repeat with remaining ham and scrambled eggs.

Put roll-ups at a shallow baking dish and broil until ham is crispy, 5 minutes.

Nutrition (per serving): 410 calories, 38 grams protein, 6 grams carbohydrates, 1 g fiber, 4 grams sugar, 26 grams fat, 13 g saturated fat, 1620 mg sodium

Immediate pot crack chicken

Yields: *4 - 6 servings*

Prep time: *0 hours 20 mins*

Total time: *1 hour 0 mins*

Ingredients

- ✓ 1 pounds. Boneless skinless chicken breasts Kosher salt
- ✓ Freshly ground black pepper 3 tablespoons. Water
- ✓ 1 (2-oz.) Packet ranch seasoning

- ✓ 1 (8-oz.) Block cream cheese, cubed 6 ounces. Shredded white cheddar
- ✓ 4 green onions, thinly sliced on a bias 8 slices cooked bacon
- ✓ Bibb lettuce, for serving

- ✓ Martin's potato rolls, for serving (optional)

Instructions

Season chicken with pepper and salt. Add chicken and water to immediate pot, then scatter in ranch seasoning and cream cheese. Seal lid and place to stress cook for 10 minutes.

Follow manufacturer's directions for rapid releasing pressure. Remove chicken breasts and then shred into balls with two forks, then blend back into cooking liquid.

Insert cheddar to close and pot lid for approximately two minutes, until cheddar is melty from residual warmth, then combine everything together.

To function as-is: crumble bacon and garnish chicken mix with green onions, crumbled bacon, and much more black pepper.

To function as a sandwich: put 1/2 cups grilled chicken mixture onto each potato roll, top with 2 loaf of bread and bibb lettuce then shut sandwich with high bun.

Yields: *1 cup*

Ingredients

- ✓ big thick-skinned cucumber

- ✓ 1 - 1/2 tbsp. White distilled vinegar 1 tsp. Kosher salt
- ✓ 1/4 tsp. Garlic powder

Instructions

Preheat oven to 225° and lightly grease 2 large baking sheet with parchment. With a mandoline or a sharp knife, cut lemon into pieces ⅛" thick.

Pat cucumbers dry with paper towels and put in a medium bowl. Add vinegar, salt, and garlic powder and then toss to blend.

Place cucumbers in an even layer on prepared baking sheets. Bake until dried, 1 hour and 30 minutes, turning halfway throughout. Eliminate sodas from menu since the beginning to crisp and let other people to retain baking.

Dinner recipes

Smashed brussels sprouts

Yields: 6 - 8 servings

Prep time: 0 hours 10 mins

Total time: 0 hours 55 mins

Ingredients

- ✓ 1 pounds. Brussels sprouts
- ✓ 2 tablespoons. Extra-virgin olive oil 2 tsp garlic, minced
- ✓ 1 tsp. Lately chopped thyme Kosher salt
- ✓ Freshly ground black pepper 1 c. Shredded mozzarella
- ✓ 1/4 c. Freshly grated parmesan Recently chopped parsley, for instance

Instructions

Preheat oven to 425° and line a large baking sheet with parchment paper. Prepare an ice bath in a big bowl.

Blanch brussels sprouts: bring a large pot of salted water to a boil. Add brussels sprouts and cook until bright green and extremely tender, 8 to 10 minutes. Add brussels sprouts into ice bath to cool then drain.

On a large baking sheet, throw blanched brussels sprouts using garlic, oil, and thyme. By the end of a little glass or mason jar, then press on brussels sprouts to smash them in a flat patty. Season every smashed brussels sprout with pepper and salt, then sprinkle mozzarella and parmesan on top.

Bake until bottoms of sprouts are crispy and cheese is melty and golden, 20 to 25 minutes.

Garnish with parsley and serve hot.

Cauliflower hash brown egg cups

Ingredients

- ✓ 1 medium head cauliflower, cut into florets and wheat 2 c. Shredded cheddar
- ✓ 14 large dinosaurs, divided 1 tsp. Garlic powder
- ✓ 1 tsp. Kosher salt

✓ 3 pieces cooked bacon, crumbled

✓ Finely chopped chives (optional), for functioning Freshly ground black pepper, for serving

Instructions

Preheat oven to 375°. Lightly grease a 12-cup muffin tin and put aside.

Drop steamed cauliflower to the bowl of a food processor and pulse until fine grains shape, no larger than the dimensions of rice.

Pour ground cauliflower onto paper towels and turn to wring out excess liquid. Do this around 3 times until cauliflower gets completely dry.

Transfer dry cauliflower to a large mixing bowl. Add cheddar, 2 greens, garlic powder, and salt and stir to blend.

Distribute mix evenly between muffin tins, about 1/4 cup per day. Use your fingers to press mixture into the sides and bottom of every cup to make nests.

Bake nests for 15 to 17 minutes until edges are golden.

Add a dab of bacon into the base of each cup and then apply egg on top, being careful to not break the yolk.

Return to oven and bake for 7 to 8 minutes longer until eggs are just set. Sprinkle with chives, pepper, and much more bacon (if wanted) prior to serving

Caprese steak

Yields: 4

Ingredients

- ✓ 3/4 c. Balsamic vinegar

- ✓ 1 teaspoon garlic, minced 2 tablespoons. Honey
- ✓ 2 tablespoons. Extra-virgin olive oil 1 tablespoon. Dried thyme
- ✓ 1 tablespoon. Dried oregano

- ✓ 4 (6-oz.) Filet mignon, or 4 big pieces of sirloin Two beefsteak tomatoes, chopped
- ✓ Kosher salt

- ✓ 4 pieces mozzarella

- ✓ Fresh basil leaves, for serving

Instructions

In a small bowl, whisk together balsamic vinegar, honey, garlic, olive oil, dried thyme, and dried oregano.

Pour over beef and let marinate 20 minutes. Season tomatoes with salt and pepper.

Heat grill to high. Grill beef 4 to 5 minutes each side, then top with mozzarella and tomatoes and cover grill until cheese is melty, 2 minutes.

Shirt with ginger before serving.

Best-ever london broil

Yields: 6 servings

Ingredients

- ✓ 1 (2-lb.) London broil top-round beef Kosher salt
- ✓ Freshly ground black pepper 1/4 c. Extra-virgin olive oil Juice of 1/2 lemon
- ✓ 2 tablespoons. Packaged brown sugar 1 tablespoon.
- ✓ Worcestershire sauce

- ✓ 4 cloves garlic, minced For the herb butter
- ✓ 1/2 c. (1 stick) butter, softened

- ✓ 1 tablespoon. Lately chopped parsley 2 tsp. Lately chopped chives
- ✓ Zest of 1/2 lemon 1/2 tsp. Kosher salt
- ✓ Pinch crushed red pepper flakes

Instructions

In a medium bowl, whisk together oil, lemon juice, brown sugar, worcestershire, and garlic.

Season beef generously with pepper and salt, then rub oil mix around. Let sit at room temperature for one hour or two up to overnight.

Preheat broiler. Brush garlic off then put beef on a sheet pan. Place pan on top rack (nearest to the heating area) and broil 6 to 7 minutes, until top is lightly bubbling. Switch and broil 4 to 5 minutes longer, until internal temperature reaches 125° (for medium rare).

Let rest 10 minutes before carving. Serve with herb butter.

Make herb butter In a small bowl, combine butter with herbs, lemon zest, salt, and red pepper flakes until smooth. Refrigerate till ready to use

Cheesesteak stuffed peppers

Yields: *4 servings*

Prep time: *0 hours 10 mins*

Total time: *0 hours 35 mins*

Ingredients

- ✓ 4 bell peppers, halved

- ✓ 1 tablespoon. Vegetable petroleum 1 big onion, sliced

- ✓ 16 oz. Cremini lettuce, chopped Kosher salt

- ✓ Freshly ground black pepper

- ✓ 1 1/2 pounds. Sirloin beef, thinly chopped 2 tsp. Italian seasoning

- ✓ 16 pieces provolone

- ✓ Recently chopped parsley, for instance

Instructions

Preheat oven to 325°. Put peppers in a large skillet and bake until tender, 30 minutes. Meanwhile, in a large skillet over medium-high warmth, heat oil. Add mushrooms and onions and season with pepper and salt. Cook till tender, 6 minutes. Insert beef and season with salt and pepper. Cook, stirring occasionally, 3 minutes. Stir in curry,

Insert provolone to underside of baked peppers and top with beef mixture. Top with a second piece of provolone and broil until golden, 3 minutes.

Garnish with parsley before serving.

Chapter five: A 7-day sample menu to the keto diet

7 DAY BALANCED KETO MEAL PLAN

Fuel & Heal Your Body With Healthy Fats

Chapter six: Tips and tricks

Is your keto diet best for you?

It's safe to state that you're keen on losing weight? Is it true to state that you're burnt out to abstains from foods which backer no or low fats and want your high fat meats? You probably could be considering moving on the keto diet, the tenderfoot. Can you wonder whether the keto diet is sheltered and right for you?

What's the ketogenic diet in any speed?

You ought to know the body uses sugar as glycogen to get the job done. The keto diet that's amazingly restricted in sugar compels your body to use fat as fuel instead of sugar, as it doesn't find enough sugar. At the stage once the body does not get sufficient sugar for fuel, the liver has been forced to change the available fat into ketones which are used by the body as fuel - hence the expression ketogenic.

This ingestion regular is really a high fat consumption routine with moderate steps of nourishment. Contingent upon your carbohydrate entrance your system arrives in a state of ketosis in under a week and stays there. As fat is used instead of sugar for fuel within the entire body, the weight loss is spectacular without a alleged restriction of calories.

The keto diet plan is together with the end aim that it you ought to mean to receive 60-

75percent of your daily calories from fat, 15-30percent from protein and only 5-10% from sugar levels.

This normally implies that you are able to eat only 20-50 grams of carbohydrates a day.

What could you be able to eat with this particular eating regimen?

The ingestion routine is a high fat eating regime which is to a level like atkins. Notwithstanding, there's more notable accentuation on fats, generally'good' fats. About the keto diet you can possess

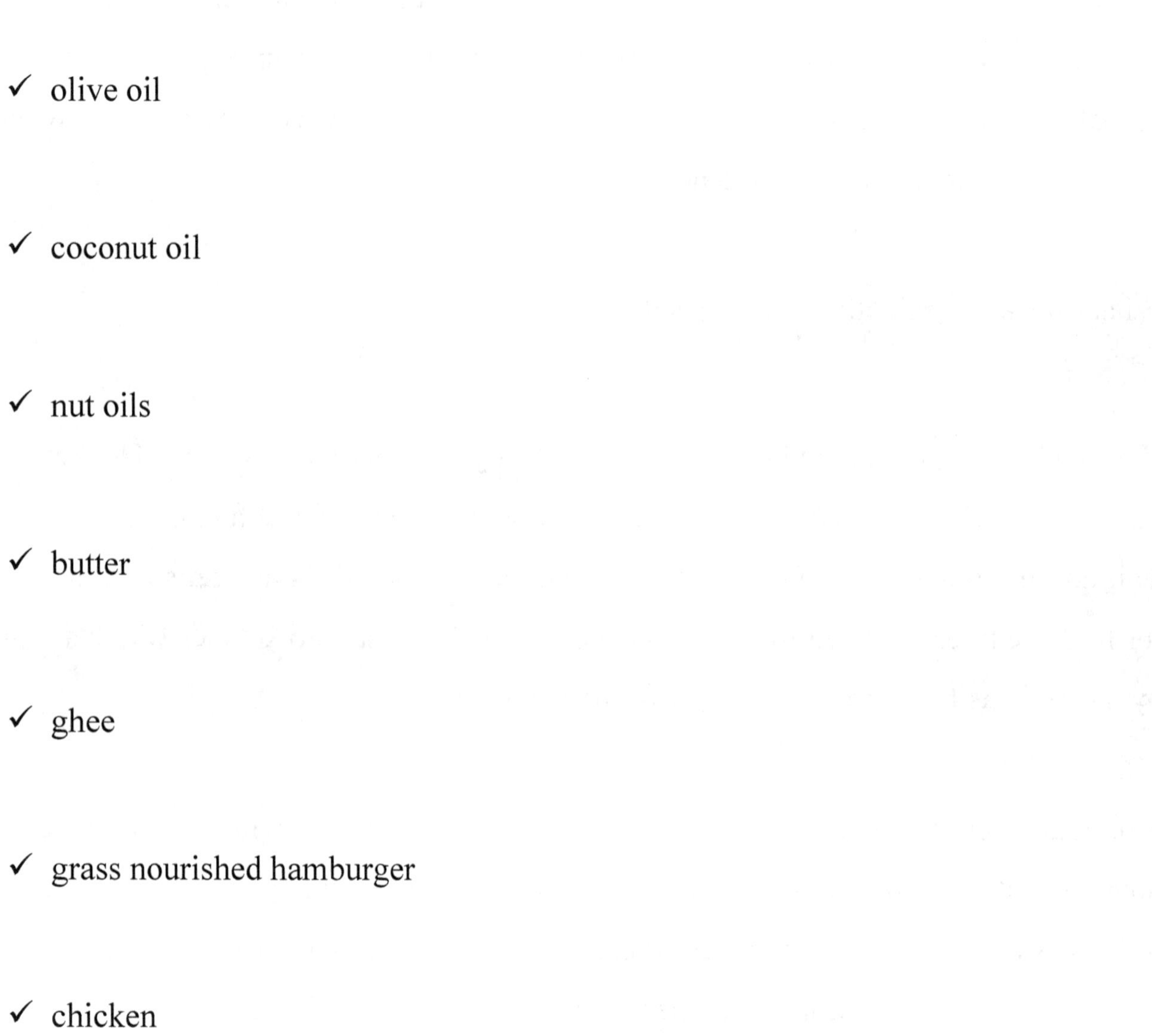

- ✓ olive oil

- ✓ coconut oil

- ✓ nut oils

- ✓ butter

- ✓ ghee

- ✓ grass nourished hamburger

- ✓ chicken

- ✓ fish

- ✓ other meats

- ✓ total fat cheddar

- ✓ eggs

- ✓ cream

- ✓ leafy greens

- ✓ non-dull veggies

- ✓ nuts

- ✓ seeds

You can similarly get an whole range of tidbits which are meant for keto devotees. As ought to be evident from this rundown, organic goods are restricted. You'll have low sugar organic goods in a restricted amount (for the most part berries), nevertheless if forego your favorite all-natural products since these are mainly sweet and also dull.

This ingestion routine comprises no carbohydrates of any type, bland vegetables such as potatoes (and all tubers), no desserts or sugar, no cakes and breads, no legumes and lentils, no pasta, no hamburgers and pizza and alongside no liquor. This also implies no espresso with milk or tea with milk - truth be told, no milk and frozen yogurts and milk based snacks.

A significant number of them have workarounds since it is possible to acquire starch free bread and pizza, you'll have cauliflower rice and currently there are cafés which take into consideration keto fans.

What are the benefits of this keto diet?

On the off chance that you're considering if this eating regimen is shielded, its defenders and the people who have achieved their weight reduction goals will favorably agree it is sheltered. One of the benefits of this keto diet you can expect:

✓ Loss of weight

✓ Reduced or no sugar spikes

✓ Appetite control

✓ Seizure controlling impact

1. Blood fat standardizes in hypertension sufferers

2. Reduced assaults of aggravation

3. Type 2 diabetes sufferers with this eating regimen may have the choice to reduce their prescriptions

4. Some advantages to people undergoing malignant growth

Besides this first four, there is not sufficient evidence to assist its viability or at any case for unique ailments as much more study is expected over the long haul.

Are there any reactions of the eating regimen?

At the stage when you initially start the keto diet, you can have the ill effects of what's called keto influenza. These signs may not occur in most individuals and for the large part start a few times in the aftermath of being to the eating regime, as soon as your body is in a state of ketosis. Some of the indicators are:

✓ nausea

✓ cramps and gut distress

- ✓ headache

- ✓ vomiting

- ✓ diarrhea or possibly blockage

- ✓ muscle cramps

- ✓ dizziness and bad concentrates on

- ✓ insomnia

- ✓ carbohydrate and glucose needs

These might take as long as seven days to expire since the human body become accustomed to the new eating system. You may likewise go through the ill effects of unique issues when you begin the keto diet - you could discover you have enlarged urine, therefore it's crucial to maintain yourself all around hydrated. You may likewise go through the ill effects of keto breath as soon as your entire body arrives in perfect ketosis and you may use a mouthwash or brush your teeth all of the more frequently.

Typically the symptoms are transitory and after your body acclimatizes to the brand new eating regimen, these should vanish.

How shielded is the keto diet?

Much the same as whatever other eating regime which restricts nourishments in explicit classes, the keto diet is not without risks. Since you should not consume lots of leafy foods, beans and lentils as well as distinct nourishments, you can have the ill effects of lack of numerous primary nutritional supplements. Considering that the eating program is packed in saturated carbohydrates and, in case you like the'bad' fats, then you can get elevated cholesterol levels raising your threat of coronary disease.

From the long haul the keto diet can similarly cause many nourishing lacks because you can not eat grains, a lot of foods developed from the floor and consume fiber as additionally important nutrients, minerals, phytonutrients and mobile reinforcements as well as other items. It's possible to go through the ill effects of gastrointestinal distress, brought down bone depth (no milk and distinct wellsprings of calcium) and liver and kidney problems (the eating routine places added pressure both organs).

Is your keto diet okay for you?

On the off chance that you're delighted to forego your normal dietary principles and are really quick to lose pounds, you may be tempted to provide a shot that the keto diet. The best problem with this particular eating regimen is lousy patient consistence due to this glucose restriction, and that means you need to be sure you may live together with your nutrition decisions. In case you basically see it too difficult to even consider after, you are able to go to a rendition of this adjusted keto diet which provides more carbohydrates.

Regardless, the keto diet is surely effective in assisting you to get more healthy. As indicated through a continuous report a high number of those heavy patients followed were successful in becoming thinner. Any problems they faced were transitory. On the off probability you don't possess some significant medical problems besides stoutness and have been unsuccessful in getting thinner following any classic eating regimen, the keto diet might be a fair option. You ought to be wholly resolved to eliminate the weight and be put up to select a restricted eating regimen as determined. Irrespective of whether you've some curative problems, you can take your primary care doctor's recommendation along with a nutritionist's leadership and proceed on this eating regimen.

Another evaluation which has been performed for a lengthier period revealed that heading to the keto diet plan is beneficial in weight loss and additionally contributes to diminished cholesterol levels using a lowering in the cholesterol and also an expansion in the fantastic cholesterol.

Is your keto diet okay for you? Most experts and nutritionists are agreed the keto diet is beneficial for weight loss reduction within the current moment. Connected to the long haul, further investigations are required. Do recall that heftiness is not an educated choice because it accompanies its danger of health care troubles.

Is it true to state that you're ideal for your keto diet?

Nowadays, it seems as if everyone is talking the ketogenic (to put it clearly, keto) diet - that the low-starch, moderate protein, high fat eating program which alters your body to a fat-copying machine. Hollywood celebrities and specialist competitions have publicly touted this current eating program's benefits, from becoming more healthy, bringing down sugar, combating aggravation, diminishing malignancy danger, expanding energy, to interrupts aging. What's keto something which you need to look at taking on? The corresponding will explain what this eating pattern is all about, the advantages and disadvantages, as the issues to cover particular head to.

What's keto?

Ordinarily, the body uses glucose as the basic wellspring of gas to get energy. At the stage when you're on a keto diet and you're ingesting not many carbohydrates with only moderate steps of nourishment (abundance protein could be altered over to carbohydrates), your system switches its own fuel source to operate normally on fat. The liver also produces ketones (a type of unsaturated fat) out of fat. These ketones turned into a gas hotspot for your own human body, especially the brain which devours a whole lot of energy and may run on either sugar or ketones.

At the stage when the entire body produces ketones, it passes a metabolic condition called ketosis. Fasting is the toughest approach to achieve ketosis. At the stage when you're eating or fasting not many carbohydrates and only moderate steps of protein, your body goes to swallowing burning fat. That's the reason people will generally shed weight on the keto diet.

Benefits of the keto diet

The keto diet is not new. It started being used throughout the 1920s as a curative remedy to deal with epilepsy in kids, however when hostile into epileptic drugs went to the current market, the ingestion routine dropped into indefinite quality to the stage. Given its accomplishment in reducing the amount of seizures in epileptic patients, progressively more study has been achieved on the potential for their eating regimen to take care of a range of neurologic problem and distinct sorts of continuous diseases.

- ✓ **neurodegenerative sicknesses.** New study shows the benefits of keto from alzheimer's, parkinson's, chemical imbalance, and many sclerosis (ms). It may likewise be defensive in horrible brain stroke and damage. 1 theory for keto's neuroprotective affects is the ketones delivered through ketosis give more fuel to synapses, which might allow those telephones to oppose the injury from aggravation caused by those disorders.

- ✓ **fat and weight loss.** From the event which you're trying to get slimmer, the keto diet is extremely successful as it helps with getting to and discard your muscle. Constant craving is the maximum issue when you try to get fit. The keto diet keeps a strategic space from this dilemma since decreasing carbohydrate utilization and enlarging fat entrance advance satiety, which makes it easier for people to hold fast to the eating regime. Within an investigation, corpulent guineas pigs lost twofold the amount of fat inside 24 weeks moving to a low-carb diet (20.7 pounds) compared with the amassing on a low-carb eating regime (10.5 pounds).

- ✓ **type two diabetes.** Apart from weight decrease, the keto diet also helps update insulin affectability, which is ideal for anyone with type two diabetes. In a test dispersed in nutrition and metabolism, experts found that girls who ate low-fat keto counts calories possess the choice to altogether reduce their dependence on diabetes and could even change it in the long term. What's more, it enriches other health markers, as an instance, bringing down triglycerides and ldl (terrible) cholesterol and increasing hdl (good) cholesterol.

- ✓ **cancer.** A excellent a lot of people don't understand that disorder cells' principle fuel is glucose. This implies eating the appropriate eating regimen might help stifle disease growth. Considering that the keto diet is very low in carbohydrates, it hastens the malignancy cells of the essential wellspring of gas, which can be sugar. At the stage once the body produces ketones, the strong cells may use that as energy yet not the disorder cells, so that they are being hungry to death. As right now as 1987, assesses on keto eats less carbohydrates have shown diminished tumor growth and enhanced endurance for a variety of malignancies.

- ✓ The key eligibility involving the keto diet and also the conventional american or paleo abstains from food is that it contains less carbohydrates and more fat. The keto diet brings about ketosis with flowing ketones running from 0.5-5.0 mm. This may be estimated using a house blood ketone display with ketone test strips. (it'd be perfect if you see that analyzing ketones in urine is not exact.)

Measure by step directions to formulate a keto diet

1. Sugars

For a fantastic many individuals, to achieve ketosis (becoming ketones over 0.5 mm) anticipates them to restrict carbs to someplace near 20-50 g (g)daily. The actual measure of carbohydrates will vary from individual to individual. For the most part, the more insulin secure someone is, the more secure they're to ketosis. Some insulin touchy competitions practicing vivaciously can devour in excess of 50 g/day and remain in ketosis, while individuals with type two diabetes and insulin resistance may should be like 20-30 g/day.

Even though discovering carbohydrates, one is allowed to use net carbohydrates, which means complete carbs less fiber and sugar alcohols. The concept of web carbs is to combine just carbs that boost insulin and glucose. Fiber does not have some hormonal or metabolic impact hence do many sugar alcohols. The particular situation is maltitol, which may have a non-unimportant impact on insulin and glucose. Along these lines, if maltitol is about the fixing record, sugar ought not be deducted from carbs that are complete.

The amount of carbohydrates you can devour and remain in ketosis can likewise change after a while contingent upon keto modification, weight loss, clinic propensities, medications, and so forth. This manner, an individual ought to gauge his/her ketone amounts on a normal assumption.

So far as the general eating routine, carb-thick nourishments such as pastas, oats, potatoes, rice, legumes, sugary desserts, soft drinks, juices, and beverage aren't affordable.

Most milk products include carbohydrates as lactose (milk sugar). Be as it may, a few have less carbohydrates and may be used consistently. These include hard cheeses (parmesan, cheddar), delicate, high-grade cheeses (brie), full-fat cream cheddar, overpowering whipping cream, and harsh cream.

A carbohydrate level beneath 50 g/day for the large part divides into the corresponding:

✓ 5-10 g carbohydrates from protein-based nourishments. Eggs, cheddar, and shellfish will extract a few lingering g of carbohydrates from routine sources and contained marinades and tastes.

✓ 10-15 g carbohydrates from non-dull vegetables.

✓ 5-10 gram carbohydrates from nuts/seeds. Most nuts feature 5 6 g carbohydrates per oz.

✓ 5-10 gram carbs from organic products, by way of instance, berries, olives, tomatoes, and avocados.

✓ 5-10 gram carbs from incidental sources, by way of instance, low-carb snacks, high fat dressings, or drinks with restricted amounts of sugar.

Drinks

The huge bulk need at any speed a massive part of a gallon of liquid daily. The best resources are sifted water, organic tea and espresso (ordinary and decaf, unsweetened), and unsweetened coconut and almond milk. Diet soft drinks and drinks are best kept a tactical space from since they include fake sugars. On the off probability that you drink white or red wine, point of confinement into 1-2 eyeglasses, the drier the better. On the off likelihood that you drink spirits, stay away in the enhanced mixed beverages.

2. Protein

A keto diet plan is certainly not a high protein diet. The explanation is that protein assembles insulin and may be altered over to sugar by means of a process called gluconeogenesis, then, repressing ketosis. Be as it may, a keto diet shouldn't be too low in protein as it can prompt reduction of muscular tissue and capability.

The normal grown-up needs about 0.8-1.5 gram per kilogram (kg) of healthy weight daily. It's crucial to create the computation determined by slim weight, not include up to body fat. The explanation is really on the reasons that fat doesn't anticipate protein to maintain, only the healthy majority.

For example, if someone gauges 150 pounds (or 150/2.2 = 68.18 kg) and contains a muscle versus fat material of 20 percent (or match pounds of 80 percent = 68.18 kg x 0.8

= 54.55 kg), the protein requirement can run from 44 (= 54.55 x 0.8) to 82 (= 54.55 x 1.5) g/day.

The people who are insulin protected or performing the keto diet for therapeutic reasons (cancerous growth, epilepsy, etc.) Should anticipate to be closer to the decrease protein limitation. So far as potential is for the people that are lively or athletic. For each other individual who's using the keto diet for weight loss reduction or alternative health benefits, the amount of day daily protein could be a location in the center.

Greatest wellsprings of excellent protein comprise:

✓ organic, fed eggs (6-8 gram of protein/egg)

✓ grass-sustained meats (6-9 gram of protein/oz)

✓ animal-based wellsprings of all omega-3 fats, by way of instance, wild-got alaskan salmon, sardines, and anchovies, and herrings. (6-9 gram of protein/oz)

✓ nuts and seeds, for instance, macadamia, almonds, walnuts, flaxseeds, hemp, and sesame seeds. (4-8 gram of protein/quarter cup)

✓ berries (1-2 gram of protein/oz)

3. Fat

Having made sense of the particular measures of carbohydrates and protein to consume, the rest of the eating regime originates from fat. A keto diet plan is basically saturated in fat. On the off chance that sufficient fat is consumed, body fat is maintained. In case that gauge hardship is needed, an individual ought to consume less dietary fat and rely on place away muscle to fat ratio for energy intake.

(as a percent of absolute caloric entrance)

______________________________maintain weight_____reduce weight Carbs_________5-10percent________________5-10percent Protein_10-15percent__________10-15percent

Fat from diet_____________70-80percent________________35-40percent

Fat from place away body fat__0 percent_________________35-40percent

For men and women that expend 2,000 calories each day to keep their weight up daily by day fat admissions stretch from approximately 156-178 g/day. For big or energetic people with higher vitality necessities that are looking after fat admissions might even exceed 300 g/day.

A fantastic many folks can endure high levels of fat, nevertheless certain conditions, as an instance, gallbladder expulsion can help determine the amount of fat which may be consumed in a lone dinner. In this instance, progressively see dinners or use of bile salts or pancreatic fats in lipase may be helpful.

Abstain from eating fats that are unwanted, by way of instance, trans fat, deeply refined polyunsaturated vegetable oils, in the same way substantial steps of omega-6 polyunsaturated fats.

Greatest nourishments to acquire excellent fats comprise:

✓ avocados and avocado oil

✓ coconuts and coconut oil

✓ grass-bolstered disperse, ghee, and hamburger fat

✓ organic, fed overpowering cream

✓ olive oil

✓ lard from fed beans

✓ medium chain triglycerides (mcts)

Mct is a particular type of fat that's processed distinctively compared to normal long-chain polyunsaturated fats. The liver may use mcts to swiftly create energy, before sugar, in this way allowing an enlarged creation of ketones.

Concentrated wellsprings of mct oil are all available as improvements. Quite a few people use them to help achieve ketosis. The major nutrients that's extremely full of mcts is coconut oil. Approximately 66 percent of this coconut fat is obtained from mct.

Who has to be cautious with a keto diet?

For the vast bulk, a keto diet is sheltered. Nevertheless, there are certain men and women who should take excellent mind and discuss with their primary care doctors prior to going on this kind of eating regimen.

- ✓ people taking prescriptions for diabetes. Measurement may ought to be balanced as sugar goes with a low-carb dietplan.

- ✓ people taking prescriptions for hypertension. Measurement may ought to be balanced because circulatory strain goes with a low-carb diet plan.

- ✓ people that are breastfeeding shouldn't go on a rigorous low-carb diet since the body can lose approximately 30 gram of carbohydrates daily by way of this milk.

This manner, have at any rate 50 gram of carbs daily whilst breastfeeding.

✓ people who have kidney disease should counselor together with their primary care doctors prior to performing a keto diet.

✓ Normal concerns using a keto diet

✓ not having the option to arrive in ketosis. Make sure you aren't eating a great deal of protein and there's no covered up carbohydrates in the bundled nourishments which you expend.

✓ eating a unsuitable forms of fat, by way of instance, the profoundly tasteful polyunsaturated corn and soybean oils.

✓ symptoms of a "keto-influenza, by way of instance, feeling dazed, dazedness, cerebral pains, fatigue, cerebrum mist, and obstruction. When in ketosis, your system will generally discharge further sodium. On the off possibility that you is not getting sufficient sodium in the eating routine, signs of a keto-influenza may appear. This can be easily cured by drinking two cups of soup (with contained salt) daily. On the off probability that you clinic vivaciously or the sweat speed is elevated, you might have to include back much more sodium.

✓ morning effect. Regular fasting blood sugars are below 100 mg/dl and also a fantastic many men and women in ketosis will reach this amount on the off probability they are not diabetic. Be as it may, in certain folks fasting blood glucose will generally increment, especially toward the start of the day, while on a keto diet. This is referred to as the"day split effect" and is due to the ordinary circadian ascent in daytime cortisol (stress hormone) that animates the liver to make more glucose. On the off probability that this happens, make certain you aren't expending excessive protein in dinner instead of very close to sleep time. Anxiety and bad rest can similarly prompt increased cortisol levels. In the event you are insulin secure, you might likewise require more chance to achieve ketosis.

✓ low athletic performance. Keto-adjustment for the most part takes about a month. During which, instead of doing exceptional exercises or planning, switch to something which is less enthused. Following the adjustment period frame, athletic implementation for the most part goes back to normal or away and far superior, especially for continuance sports.

✓ keto-rash is certainly not a standard symptom of this eating routine. Probably explanations incorporate creation of ch3)2co (a sort of ketone) from the sweat that disturbs skin or supplement insufficiencies such as minerals or protein. Shower following action and make sure you eat supplement thick whole nourishments.

✓ ketoacidosis. That is an exceptionally rare condition that occurs when blood ketone levels go over 15 mm. A well-figured keto diet does not result in ketoacidosis. Certain conditions, as an instance, type 1 diabetes, being on meds using sglt-2 inhibitors for type 2 diabetes, or breastfeeding require extra attentive. Side effects include laziness, illness, heaving, and rapid shallow calming. Mild cases could be settled using sodium bicarbonate mixed in with diminished orange or squeezed apple. Intense unwanted effects need brief medicinal thought.

Can be keto safe for long-term?

This is a place of a disagreement. Regardless of the fact that there have never been any investigations demonstrating any long haul consequences of being to a keto diet, a lot of specialists now accept the body may develop an"obstruction" to the benefits of ketosis except when a person routinely cycles throughout it. Additional eating a high fat eating regimen from the long haul might not be sensible for many body types.

Patterned keto diet

When you can create over 0.5 mm of ketones in the bloodstream onto a dependable assumption, the time has come to start reintroducing carbs once again in the eating regimen. Instead than eating only 20-50 gram of carbs/day, you may have to enlarge it to 100-150 gram on these carb- nourishing days. Often, 2-3 times per week will be adequate. In a perfect world, this can be also achieved on quality preparing days where you actually increment your protein entrance.

This methodology of biking can produce the eating regular arrangement adequate to particular people that are reluctant to for many time kill some of their favored nourishments. Whatever the instance, it may additionally bring down function and assure into the keto diet or activate gorges in vulnerable men and women.

Should girls prevent the keto diet?

The keto diet has become a serious well-known stage in the health network. It's been proven to assist in the reduction of weight and also bringing the aggravation in the intestine. New study has indicated beneficial consequences for the 2 folks sticking to some keto fashion diet.

What's the keto diet?

First, a keto, or ketogenic diet, is meant to maintain your body into a larger level a ketosis condition. Ketosis is not irregular. This is where your body is reduced on sugar. At the stage when this occurs, it starts to consume fat, instead of the carbohydrates. The process produces ketones. The standard individual does not stay in a ketogenic state besides throughout exercise that is substantial, as an instance, crossfit, or even while pregnant.

A ketogenic diet improvements exceptionally low sugar and high fat entrance. The body will consequently, use fat to make energy. This eating regimen has additionally been looked to reduce immune system disorders, endocrine disorders, and also has cancerous growth fighting properties.

Ketosis is an issue with diabetics. This sometimes happens if not using enough insulin.
How can keto benefit crossfit competitions?
As expressed earlier, a ketogenic diet aids with absorbing fat, like this becoming more healthy. This low-carb diet is similar to the paleo diet. We're a good defender of paleo about the grounds that it progresses greater protein for fuel instead of carbs. As we voiced previously, the keto diet uses fat instead of protein to fuel. A keto and paleo diet consume fat whilst appearing after muscle.

A competitor practicing in a heightened level, by way of instance, crossfit, will see enlarged fat and energy misfortune, without decreasing bulk.

For what reason is your keto diet helpful for women?

The benefits of being a woman on this eating regimen are amazingly acceptable. Regardless of the weight loss and muscle improve, a keto diet includes a stunning way of assisting the endocrine system. We as a whole understand the effect hormones have about the woman competitor.

Fluctuating hormones may cause distress, fatigue, and sometimes even gloom. The link among hormones and cancerous growth can not be refused. A keto diet also has emerged to each of the more inclined guide the endocrine frame. As a result, it reduces the frequency of particular cancers, thyroid malady, and even diabetes.

How can a women begin a keto diet?

Gradually and carefully. A keotgenic diet shouldn't be started in an whole 100 percent. You need to slowly decrease the amount of carbohydrates you expend. Cutting the carbohydrates too quickly can truly have a negative effect. It may pressure the human body and befuddle that, hence causing a crazy unevenness.

Furthermore, if pregnant or nursing, you shouldn't use a keto diet. In this age, eat a balanced eating regimen of organic goods, veggies, milk, and grains.

My very best advice, get your own body as steady as can be enabled, and then gradually combine a ketogenic diet.

Keto dieting? Here are 10 foods you should get on your own kitchen

The ketogenic diet is a very fruitful health improvement program. It utilizes high fat and low carb fixings in order to consume fat instead of sugar. A lot of people know about the atkins diet, no matter how the keto plan restricts carbohydrates more.

Since we're surrounded by push joints and ready dinners, it is inclined to be an evaluation to steer clear of carb-rich nourishments, nevertheless proper organizing can help.

Plan snacks and menus at any speed seven days, which means you aren't gotten with only large carbohydrate feast choices. Research keto plans online; there are several acceptable ones to navigate. Inundate yourself at the keto manner of life, find your favorite strategies, and stick together.

You will find a few items which are principles of a keto diet. Make sure to have these items shut by:

1. Eggs - employed in omelets, quiches (really, substantial lotion is valid on keto!), challenging bubbled as a tidbit, low carb pizza out layer, and that is just the start; in case you enjoy eggs, you've got an extraordinary chance of achievement with this eating regimen

2. Bacon - can I want an excuse? Breakfast, plate of mixed greens include, hamburger topper, blt's (no bread clearly; try a blt in a bowl, then hurled in mayo)

3. Cream cheddar - dozens of programs, pizza outsides, principle dishes, pastries

4. Shredded cheddar - sprinkle over taco beef in a bowl, made into tortilla leads the microwave, plate of mixed greens toppers, low-fat pizza and enchiladas

5. A great deal of romaine and spinach - fill up about the green vegetables; possess bounty accessible for a quick serving of mixed greens if food cravings struck

6. Ez-sweetz liquid sugar - use 2 or more three drops rather than sugar; this sugar that is counterfeit has become the most feature and demanding to use that I have discovered

7. Cauliflower - new or solidified sacks you're able to consume this low carb veggie without anybody else, hurled in olive oil and ready, crushed in salads that are imitation, cleaved/destroyed and used rather than rice beneath principle dishes, in low fat and keto pizza coverings, and much more

8. Frozen chicken strips - have a massive pack near by; defrost quickly and barbecue, saute, mix in with vegetables and top with garlic sauce at a low-carb flatbread, utilize in chicken piccata, chicken alfredo, tacos, enchiladas, indian butter chicken, and that is just the tip of this iceberg

9. Ground beef - create a significant hamburger and shirt with a vast selection of items from cheddar, to sauteed mushrooms, to fire broiled onions... Or on the flip side outwards and cook together with taco flavoring and utilize provolone cheddar taco shells; chuck in a dish with avocado, lettuce, cheddar, acrid lotion to get a tortilla-less taco serving of mixed greens

10. Almonds (plain or seasoned) - those are a tasty and strong tidbit; nonetheless, make sure to think about them you consume, in light of how the carbohydrates do contain. Flavors include habanero, coconut, vinegar and salt and then a few.

The keto program is an elastic and intriguing way to get slimmer, with heaps of celestial nourishment choices. Keep these 10 items provided on your fridge, cooler, and larder, and you will be ready to put together some yummy keto snacks and dishes instantly.

The ketogenic diet is a good selection for any person who wants to have thinner. Go to the nutritious keto website, a significant advantage in which keto calorie counters might access to dinner ideas and keto diet myths.

Conclusion

Keto is an eating routine that needs cutting carbohydrates and fats that are expanding together with the target of assisting the body absorb its own fat stores each of the more efficiently. Ketogenic eats less are useful due to and large health and becoming healthier. Prominently, ketogenic abstains from meals have helped particular people shed undesirable muscle without intense yearnings which are normal of distinct weight control programs. It is also been found that a couple of people with type two diabetes may use keto as a way to restrain their unwanted side effects. No matter if keto is right for you depends upon various components. Assuming you do not go through the ill effects of healthcare difficulties, a ketogenic diet may provide a lot of benefits, especially for weight loss reduction. The most important situation to recollect would be to consume an unbelievable parity of veggies, lean beef, and organic carbs.

Basically adhering to whole nourishments is probably the most effective procedures for eating ardently, basically about the grounds that it is a supportable strategy.

It is crucial to take note of this a lot of research shows ketogenic slims down really are tough to stay with. Therefore, the very best advice is to find a solid way of eating that works for you. It is okay to try new things, just don't jump in mind first. Greatest weight loss workouts for girls Wlose weight on keto for women more than 50hile that the keto diet provides numerous benefits in weight loss and by and large health, it is in each situation better to combine diet with workout. From formula notions to exercise programs, you will have the choice to test out our fit mother preparing for three times of drive.

The entirety of our arrangements are designed for active mothers just like you. No injury eats less carbohydrates, no 3-hour exercises.

Just science-supported principles that will aid you with feeling the best you've got in years.

CPSIA information can be obtained
at www.ICGtesting.com
Printed in the USA
BVHW050955110621
609348BV00014B/1812